T0329960

Dynamics of the Firm

Dynamics of the Firm

Strategies of Pricing and Organisation

Edited by

John Groenewegen
Erasmus University,
Group for Research and Advice in
  Strategic Management and Industrial
  Policy (GRASP),
Rotterdam, The Netherlands

Edward Elgar

Published by
Edward Elgar Publishing Limited
Gower House
Croft Road
Aldershot
Hants GU11 3HR
England

Edward Elgar Publishing Company
Old Post Road
Brookfield
Vermont 05036
USA

British Library Cataloguing in Publication Data
Dynamics of the Firm: Strategies of
Pricing and Organisation
   I. Groenewegen, John
   338.5

Library of Congress Cataloguing in Publication Data
Dynamics of the firm: strategies of pricing and organisation / edited
   by John Groenewegen
         p.   cm.
    "On 13 Nov. 1992 The Dutch Association of Post Keynesian Studies
organised its 13th annual conference on the 'Dynamics of the Firm'" –
–CIP galley.
    Includes bibliographical references and index.
    1. Transaction costs—Congresses.   2. System analysis—Congresses.
3. Industrial organization (Economic theory)—Congresses.
4. Pricing—Congresses.   5. Business enterprises—Case studies–
–Congresses.   I. Groenewegen, John, 1949–
HB846.3.D95   1993
338.5—dc20   93–24565
                                        CIP

ISBN 978-1-85278-934-3

Printed and bound by CPI Group (UK) Ltd, Croydon, CR0 4YY

Contents

Figures

Tables

Contributors

Bart Nooteboom is Professor of Management and Organisation at the University of Groningen.

Fred Lee lectures in the Department of Economics at De Montfort University, Leicester.

F. Gregory Hayden is Professor of Economics at the University of Nebraska in Lincoln.

Kurt Stephenson lectures in the Department of Economics at the University of Nebraska in Lincoln.

John Groenewegen is Associate Professor of Economics and Modern Japan Studies at the Erasmus University Rotterdam and Director of GRASP.

Paul Merkelbach is at Philips Electronics and Professor of Economics at Erasmus University Rotterdam.

Frans Buelens lectures in the Department of Economics at the University of Antwerp.

Jan Donders is deputy managing director of the Directorate of General Policy Coordination of the Directorate General of Industry of the Ministry of Economic Affairs in the Netherlands.

Eric van Kooij is a Policy Planning Officer at the Directorate General of Industry of the Ministry of Economic Affairs in the Netherlands.

Acknowledgements

This publication and its preparatory conference of the Dutch Association of Post Keynesian Studies could not have been realised without the financial support of the Faculty of Economics of the Erasmus University Rotterdam, the 'Vereniging Trust Funds' of Erasmus University Rotterdam and the Group for Research and Advice in Strategic Management and Industrial Policy (GRASP).

Many thanks to the authors for bearing with editorial requests and meeting deadlines so efficiently.

A very special word of thanks to Wilma Speijer and Johan Polder for turning manuscripts into a camera-ready copy.

Introduction: Towards A Theory of the Dynamics of the Firm?

John Groenewegen

In this introductory chapter I will discuss the dynamics of the firm from a theoretical point of view and show how the chapters in this volume contribute to a better understanding of the dynamics of firms.

THEORIES OF THE FIRM

A theory of the firm should provide concepts which can be operationalised for the description, understanding and explanation of firms. Theory should provide an explanation of the existence as well as the dynamics of economic organisation in general and of the firm in particular.

Traditional neoclassical theory of the firm is limitly useful, because firms are not endogenous, but production functions showing the relation between output and inputs. These 'firms' operate in a given and static environment. Given the market structure, given maximising behaviour and given the technology, what then will be the optimal combination of production factors? In fact only the minimum efficient scale (MES) explains the size of firms.

Agency theory is another branch of theory worthy of mention here. It is of the 'mechanistic design'-type, in which agents can specify ex ante monitoring and incentive devices in such a way that violation of contracts will be minimised. The actors are neoclassical maximisers using opportunism (cheating) to realise their goals. Agency theory builds complex models with time lags, asymmetric information and the like, but its relevance to understanding and explaining firms is doubtful (Arrow, 1985).

In relation to agency theory the firm as a nexus of contracts should be mentioned. In a perfectly symmetrical relationship employers (principals) negotiate with employees (agents) about the contracts, in which the transaction of labour is coordinated. Alchian and Demsetz (1972) explain how in team production the monitor has to prevent agents from shirking and how competition among monitors will prevent them from exploiting agents. Actors are assumed to be fully informed about prices, marginal productivities and the like and they are able to exit and renegotiate until equilibria result. Agency theory lacks the translation to empirical situations; the approach constructs impressive models which are unfortunately not very useful for understanding real organisations.

An important step forward in the theory of the firm was made by Williamson (1975, 1985). Institutional economics in general and the transaction cost economics (TCE) of Williamson in particular provide some very useful concepts and insights for understanding and explaining the firm. The central problem definition is the organisation of transactions. Why is, for instance, the transaction of capital coordinated in external capital markets, but also in internal 'miniature' markets of the M-form? Why is the transaction of labour coordinated in external labour markets, and also in internal labour markets? In his theoretical framework Williamson developed four categories of governance structures (market-, bi-, tri- and unified governance), which he matched with categories of transactions (degree of asset specificity, frequency and uncertainty). Different types of contracts (classical, neoclassical and relational) are linked with the governance structures. TCE has proven to be very useful for characterising transactions and for a first understanding of the appropriate governance structures. 'Appropriate' here means 'efficient' and that brings us to the main issue in TCE: although Williamson admits that explanatory variables other than efficiency can play a role (especially in the organization of work). It is his strong conviction that economic efficiency is the most important explanatory variable for understanding and explaining firms. A selection process is assumed to be at work taking care of the survival of the fittest. Critics have extensively discussed this Darwinian element in TCE and also its functionalism has been the subject of debate (Dow, 1987; Hodgson, 1988). Beside that critics have also pointed to the static nature of TCE, a characteristic of special interest for the topic of this volume (for an overview see Pitelis, 1991).

Williamson has presented his TCE as a comparative institutional analysis. After a description of the characteristics of the transaction (asset specifity, opportunism and the like), Williamson shows the difficulties in drafting and monitoring market contracts which offers an opportunity for more efficient governance structures like firms of different structures (U-form, M-form, conglomerate, transnational corporations and the like). Governance structures exist because others fail due to relatively high production and transaction costs. This approach is static: given the technology, given the asset specificity, given opportunism and given the other variables in the 'organizational failures framework', which organizational structure is most efficient then? The question how governance structures develop over time is not at stake. Apart from the so-called 'fundamental transition' of a market with a large number of suppliers to a situation of small numbers, dynamics is no part of TCE.

THE IMPORTANCE OF STRATEGIES

Strategic behaviour does not play a role in TCE. Like in neoclassical theory agents have only one option: to select the most efficient organisation. As far as strategy is discussed the relation is one of strategy resulting from structure and not Chandler's 'strategy causes structure'. Williamson presents strategy as the result of structure, for example in his analysis of the size of the U-form (structure) causing the strategy to construct the M-form.

Clearly, for explaining the dynamics of firms an understanding of the strategies of firms is crucial for strategies aim at the change of organizational structures. Strategies of firms are not developed in a vacuum of institution free markets where objectively efficient structures can be or are selected. On the contrary, understanding strategies of firms demands an analysis, in which the firm is considered as 'embedded' in an environment. After we have discussed this embeddedness, we will turn our attention to the ingredients of a theoretical framework appropriate for understanding the dynamics of firms.

Grabner (1993, p. 1) discusses the neoclassical utilitarian tradition as one that focusses on 'the individual grains in the fuzzy picture of social reality, namely on the atomized actors'. Such a focus can offer detailed images of grains, but will mostly not provide a more or less clear picture of the whole. The atomisation of actors is predominant in the theories of the firm discussed above, in other words: the actors are 'under-socialised'. Granovetter (1985) explained that both undersocialisation and 'oversocialisation' (norms determine behaviour) result in atomised actors, which are isolated from their immediate social context. Both under- and oversocialisation should be avoided and replaced by the embeddedness approach. "Embeddedness' refers to the fact that economic action and outcomes, like all social action and outcomes, are affected by actors' dyadic relations and by the structure of the overall network of relations' (Grabner, 1993, p.4). Theories with atomised actors do not provide the concepts for understanding (changes in) behaviour nor do they provide concepts for understanding the influence of actors on the environment out of which new organisational structures can arise. What seems to be appropriate is an approach in which the environment influences behaviour on the one hand and in which behaviour can influence the environment on the other. Within that framework actors develop strategies in which a change of the environment (market structure as well as socio-political structure) can be part. Embeddedness implies that firms operate in a system of values, norms and rules, that they have developed routinized behaviour and that network relations with for instance labour unions, government, research institutes and the like are important for understanding the strategies of specific firms. Markets then have to be conceived of as 'institutionalised' markets where the separation between markets and hierarchies is not so clear at all. Between markets and hierarchies are grey areas where organisational structures arise, change and disappear in processes of change and evolution. In the empirical world theoretical governance structures are penetrated with elements of other governance structures as explained so well in Imai and Itami (1984). Hodgson (1988) discusses the same issue as the 'impurity principle' meaning that a variety of institutional forms exist in market economies and that hierarchies certainly do not always replace markets, but are often supplements of markets resulting in mixed modes, in which elements of different theoretical types are combined. This is also convincingly explained in Stinchcombe (1990), where it is shown that contracts can be very 'market like', but also very 'hierarchical'.

To conclude: a theoretical framework useful for analysing the dynamics of firms should consider the firm as embedded in a multi-dimensional environment within which the firm interacts. The atomistic agent should be replaced by a socialised agent in order to understand the strategies which have an impact on the dynamics of the firm.

As explained elsewhere (Dankbaar, Groenewegen and Schenk, 1990, chapter 1) the focus on conduct brings the analysis to slippery ground. Opening the box of behaviour opens the possibility for all kind of strategies depending on more or less objective factors like the market structure, but also on more subjective factors like corporate culture, relations of trust and the like. How to build a theory in such an open ended situation?

TOWARDS A THEORY OF THE DYNAMICS OF FIRMS?

Pitelis (1991) points to some important building blocks of a theory of the dynamics of firms. In market economies firms further profits through increasing the labour productivity by technological and organisational changes. So the change of for instance the putting-out systems to capitalistic manufacturing in large plants, as well as the change from a U-form to an M-form are attempts by principals to increase profits through the increase of labour productivity. Pitelis (1991) also points to another well accepted strive for profits: competition among rivals forces firms to cut costs. In the short run this can be realised through economies of scale, scope, efficient organisation and the like, in the long run through the expansion of markets, which brings us to the concept of power. In order to secure profits in the future firms need to be well informed about market developments, competitors' strategies, changes in government policies and so on. However, being well informed is not sufficient. Firms also want to control markets in order to secure future profits. Control can be realised through strategies of expansion, vertical integration, diversification, decentralisation with subcontracting and cooperation with rivals (strategic alliances and cartels).

Clearly efficiency is an important variable for understanding the existence and organisation of firms and TCE has made an important contribution to the understanding of increasing efficiency through the different organisation of transactions. Clearly of equal importance is the strive for long term profits resulting in strategies to increase labour productivity, to expand markets, to control resources, to control competitors, to control governments and the like. In short, according to Pitelis (1991), efficiency and power should be considered as two sides of the same coin. The increase of efficiency through the internalisation of the labour markets increases for instance the power of the principals over the agents, in the same way as decentralisation with subcontracting can change a hierarchy into a more powerful 'hierarchy' (Amin and Dietrich, 1991). So efficiency and power are '(....) not two different explanations of the existence of the firm, but differences in emphasis concerning two sides of the more general objective and reason for the existence of firms, the furtherance of profits for the principals' (Pitelis, 1991, 33). In other words, an explanation of the dynamics of the embedded firm asks for the application of uni-dimensional theories to be discontinued besides TCE-like efficiency approaches sociological power approaches should also be taken into account. An appropriate framework does not present actors as atomistic agents, but as socialised agents making decisions under

conditions of uncertainty operating in interaction with their economic and
socio-political environment. Research must show why (objectives) and
how (strategies) entrepreneurs organise markets as they do. This should
be done with a general theoretical framework consisting of the building
blocs of efficiency and power. Such a theoretical framework has to be
always operationalised for specific cases, in which the conditions of time
and place differ. An embedded approach implies the incorporation of
specific conditions into the analysis. Why, for example, is the capital
market not extensively internalised in Japan, when the same transaction
in the US is mainly coordinated inside the hierarchy? The reasons for
this seem to be the existence of industrial groups and relations of trust
among firms and group banks. Without that specific knowledge it is not
possible to understand the structure and dynamics of Japanese firms. A
full understanding demands a study of the embedded firm. A general
one-dimensional theory of the firm explaining the dynamics of firms in
all places and periods of history is an illusion. What hopefully can be
offered is a framework consisting of different building blocks with
concepts that can be operationalised for firms embedded in different
situations of time and place.

13TH CONFERENCE OF THE DUTCH ASSOCIATION OF POST KEYNESIAN ECONOMICS

In this volume the authors of the different chapters deal with issues of
the dynamics of firms. Some discuss theoretical issues, others focus on
empirical data or policy questions. The chapters are the edited papers of
the 13th conference of the Dutch Association of Post Keynesian
Economics held in Rotterdam 1992.

Bart Nooteboom discusses in chapter 1 the characteristics of TCE and
makes a comparison with the network approach. So here an attempt is
made to integrate efficiency, trust and power. He discusses the
epistomologal differences between the two schools of thought and shows
how TCE and network theory could be integrated into a dynamic theory
of the firm. Both power and efficiency have to be dealt with.

Another important theoretical issue in respect to the dynamics of firms
is their pricing strategy. In neoclassical theory prices and markets are
completely separated from the hierarchies. In the empirical world
however prices, power, trust and the like are combined in different ways.
Fred Lee discusses in chapter 2 Post Keynesian price theories. Three
price setting strategies are distinguished: mark up, normal cost and target
rate pricing. The three procedures are discussed and critisised in relation

to empirical studies in order to provide an empirically grounded pricing model.

In respect to empirical studies of the dynamics of the firm F. Gregory Hayden and Kurt Stephenson discuss in chapter 3 an important element of network theory. In a detailed case study the interlocks between corporations in the state of Nebraska, US is analysed. Power relations are made visible, which is an important step forward in network analysis. The authors generalise their case study into guidelines for similar studies and also translate their findings into policy recommendations.

In the following three chapters more specific issues of the dynamics of firms are discussed. In chapter 4 John Groenewegen discusses the dynamics of the Japanese firm. Special attention is paid to the characteristics of business groups. Besides efficiency and power also trust plays an important role. Firms inside these groups experience important changes: life time employment and the seniority principle are threatened. The roles of banks and General Trading Companies as well as subcontracting are reconsidered. In chapter 5 Paul Merkelbach discusses the restructuring of Philips in relation to internal and external developments. The development of a national firm into a transnational one is presented, the pressures from the market of electronics are outlined and special attention is paid to the so-called 'Centurion Operation' aiming at restructuring Philips. Frans Buelens uses the case of the Belgium holding *Société Générale* to show the power of firms towards government and to discuss the issues of a take over fight.

The dynamics of firms should have implications for government policies; especially in respect to industrial policies government should realise that policies formerly linked to sectors and specific firms need a change in focus because the structure of firms has changed. Jan Donders and Eric van Kooij discuss Dutch industrial policies and raise the question of what the policy consequences should be when vertically structured hierarchies change into network firms.

REFERENCES

Alchian, A.A. and H. Demsetz (1972), 'Production, Information Costs, and Economic Organization', *American Economic Review*, pp. 777-795.

Amin, A. and M. Dietrich (1991), 'From Hierarchy to 'Hierarchy': The Dynamics of Contemporary Corporate Restructuring in Europe', in A. Amin and M. Dietrich (ed.). *Towards A New Europe?* Aldershot: Edward Elgar Publishing, 49-73.

Arrow, K.J. (1985), 'The Economics of Agency', in W. Pratt and R. Zeckhauser (eds.). *Principals and Agents: The Structure of Business,* Boston: Harvard

Business School.

Dankbaar, B. J. Groenewegen and H. Schenk (eds.) (1990), *Perspectives in Industrial Organization*. Dordrecht: Kluwer Academic Publishers.

Dow, G.K. (1987), 'The Function of Authority in Transaction Cost Economics', *Journal of Economic Behaviour and Organization*, 8, 13-38.

Grabner, G. (1993), *The Embedded Firm; On the Socioeconomics of Industrial Networks*, London: Routledge.

Granovetter, M. (1985), 'Economic Action and Social Structure: The Problem of Embeddedness', *American Journal of Sociology*, 3, Nov., 481-450.

Hodgson, G.M. (1988), *Economics and Institutions*. Oxford: Polity Press.

Imai, K. and H. Itami (1984), 'Interpenetration of Organization and Market', *International Journal of Industrial Organization*, 2, 285-310.

Pitelis, Chr. (1991), *Market and Non-Market Hierarchies*, Oxford: Blackwell.

Stinchcombe, A.L. (1990), *Information and Organizations*, Oxford: University of California Press.

Williamson, O.E. (1975), *Markets and Hierarchies: Analysis and Antitrust Implications*. New York: The Free Press.

Williamson, O.E. (1985), *The Economic Institutions of Capitalism*. New York: The Free Press.

1. Networks and Transactions: Do They Connect?

Bart Nooteboom

INTRODUCTION

In this chapter the firm is discussed in a strategic context, from which follows the necessity of outsourcing activities. The central question in this contribution concerns the theoretical framework necessary to study interfirm relations. It is argued that in addition to transaction cost economics, network concepts also offer useful perspectives which should and can be integrated.

Transaction Cost Economics (TCE) and network concepts, as developed by the Industrial Marketing Purchasing Group (IMP), offer different approaches to issues of interfirm relations. TCE derives from neoclassical economics and is oriented towards efficiency in a static framework. IMP takes a more sociological perspective, being oriented towards the development of competence in a dynamic framework. TCE focuses on opportunism, while IMP focuses on trust. TCE concentrates on risks of dependence; IMP on opportunities for cooperation. It is argued here that both approaches offer useful perspectives and that they should and can be integrated.

STRATEGIC CONTEXT

For the sake of efficiency but also for strategic reasons, firms increasingly need to contract out activities and to seek cooperation with other firms. For the sake of efficiency, this is because outside producers who are specialised and are stimulated by market incentives will often produce more efficiently than producers who are fully integrated in the

9

user firm. For strategic reasons this is because, in order to survive in the race for low costs, high quality, innovation and flexibility in increasingly international markets, firms should concentrate on activities in which they are particularly strong in order to establish a competitive advantage. Activities need to be contracted out even when they are close to the core activities of the firm and make the contractor dependent on outside suppliers. The underlying dynamics involved are outlined in Figure 1.1.

Outsourcing is required because of the need to concentrate on core activities. This arises from the neccessity to pay more attention to R&D, to specialise and to ensure flexibility. More R&D is required with respect to its volume, effectiveness and speed, because of shortening product life cycles and the need to create enhanced quality. This latter requirement also necessitates specialisation. The need for flexibility arises from the shortening of product life cycles and fast technical advance, while developments in information and communication technology (ICT) enable more flexibility (for example, in diversified manufacturing and faster response to market developments).

The shortening of product life cycles arises from the demand for more differentiated products based on the diversity of conduct within cultures, the technical possibilities to differentiate products at lower cost as a result of ICT, and the incentive to differentiate products in order to escape from price competition. The latter reflects a general increase in competition, which in turn is due to the internationalisation of markets. This in turn is possibly the result of a certain homogenisation of consumer conduct across cultures, stemming from worldwide communication based on ICT. Also, from the supply side there is pressure to expand markets internationally in order to reach a sufficient sales volume to achieve economies of scale in spite of product differentiation and specialisation. These developments in consumer behaviour appear paradoxical: on the one hand, differentiation on the level of the individual within countries and, on the other, more similarity in lifestyles across countries. Cooperation with other firms is needed to focus on core activities, to contract out more activities (even if they are 'sensitive'), and because of the limited capability to satisfy the need to change one's own organisation. There is an increased need to retrain staff and to adapt organisations, both as a result of the need for flexibility and as a result of demographic developments (as the proportion of older people with outdated skills increases). Since there is a limit to the ability of organisations to change, more use should be made of outside capabilities.

Figure 1.1 Dynamics in the environment of firms

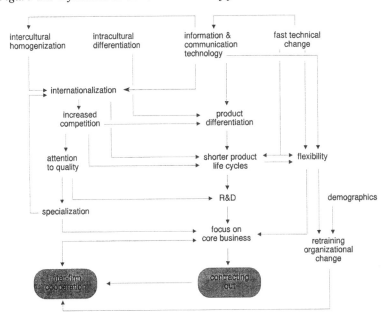

RESEARCH ISSUES

Crucial questions now arise:

.   what specifically are the advantages and the risks of contracting out?
.   under what precise conditions should activities be contracted out?
.   how can supplier-contractor relations be 'governed' in order to maximise benefits and minimise risks?

For scholars in economics and business the problem is what theory can be used to guide the search for answers to these questions. In the literature there are two schools of thought that claim to provide the required theoretical basis.

One school of thought is found in what may be called the 'network approach', associated with the IMP Group in Manchester (Cunningham, Turnbull) and particularly in Uppsala (Håkansson, 1982, 1987; Johanson and Mattson, 1985, 1987).[1] The second school of thought is 'transaction cost economics' (TCE) inspired by Coase (1937) and developed mainly by Williamson (1975, 1985).

While the two schools both appear to relate to the issues at hand, they apparently have nothing in common. The two schools hardly recognise one another as relevant, and each tends to ignore the other. This is hardly surprising, since TCE is firmly embedded in neoclassical economics, in spite of its emphasis on bounded rationality and imperfect and asymmetric information, while the IMP approach bases itself on social exchange and thereby is part of sociology rather than economics. Economics and sociology do not mix well.[2]

The ideas presented in this chapter are part of a programme that can be summarised by the following propositions:[3]

1. TCE and the IMP approach both have relevant and valuable insights to offer;
2. both have important blind spots;
3. with proper extensions of theory they can be seen to be complementary;
4. the integration of the two approaches requires an interface between sociology and economics;
5. the core of this integration or interface is the application of new (postmodern) epistemology.

The fourth proposition indicates that the realisation of the programme is a tall order. But the integration of economics and sociology is necessary for other reasons as well. When the present attention in economics to problems of bounded rationality is carried through consistently, the need for recognition of contemporary developments in epistemology will become apparent. This will provide a perspective, and indeed the need, for integrating economics and sociology.

TRANSACTION AND RELATION

A useful starting point is the comparison between TCE and the IMP approach given by Johanson and Mattson (1987). In the summary in Table 1.1 we adopt important elements from their comparison, but rephrase terms and include some modifications and additions to meet our present purposes.

The differences can be summed up as follows: TCE is oriented towards efficiency, given certain competences, and IMP is oriented towards competence building. The associated most fundamental differences are the first three and the last one. The first three can be summarised as follows: IMP is historical and TCE is not. IMP views transactions as embedded in relations that develop through time. Exchange leads to mutual adaptation, which entails investment in a relation. As a result of this, bonding between the actors develops; trust is generated, and a lasting relation emerges.

Table 1.1 Comparison between TCE and IMP

TCE	IMP
EFFICIENCY	COMPETENCE BUILDING
static	dynamic
equilibrium	social change
transactional events	transaction relation
governance structure	mutual adaptation
transactions as operations	transactions as investments
opportunism is basic	trust is basic
bounded rationality	learning
dependence as threat	dependence as bonding
dyadic transactions	multiple dyads → networks

Source: Adapted from Johanson and Mattson (1987).

Also, from the perspective of IMP, the primary value of transaction relations lies in the complementarity of knowledge, competence and access to other resources. This suggests that different firms, with different histories in different contexts of markets and technologies, have developed different perspectives and competences that cannot easily or instantaneously be adopted or transferred. Therefore, linkages with other firms are sought to gain access to competences lacking in one's own firm. In TCE the advantage of outside sourcing lies in the mobilisation of market incentives, with specialisation seen only as a means to achieve economies of scale, as a source of efficiency. The latter view of specialisation is much more limited than the view in IMP, in that the tacit assumption, typical of neo-classical economics, is that perception, knowledge and competence are not path dependent but are objective and 'given'; they are available like goods on a shelf in the shop of technology, to be acquired instantaneously at the going price. This difference between IMP and TCE is crucial since it is based on different theories of knowledge (epistemologies). We will return to that later.

Another basic difference is that in contrast to TCE, IMP looks at indirect relations (with partners of partners), which yield access to further resources. This provides an important constraint on the isolated evaluation of bilateral exchange. One should not break off a relation without considering the possible loss of indirect access to resources by way of that relation. One may chop off not just a twig but the tree of which one is oneself only a twig. This further contributes to bonding.

IMP contributes an historical, dynamic, social dimension which is lacking in TCE. Standard TCE (as formulated by Williamson) does not consider the development of perceptions of utility and opportunism as the outcome of ongoing transactions. Like neoclassical economics in general, TCE is in the habit of taking preferences, capabilities, knowledge and perception as 'stable', and as given exogenously and objectively as 'underlying realities'. IMP, on the other hand, considers differences in perception and knowledge between agents and learning by agents as a crucial dimension of transactions. While in his earlier work Williamson recognised a dimension of 'atmosphere' in transactions, which presumably might be related to 'trust', in his later work this has seemed to drop out. Without doubt, IMP has contributed a dimension which is important and crucially lacking in TCE. While TCE focuses on issues of efficiency, in a static context of given technology and competence, IMP considers competence building in a dynamic context of learning.

However, in turning away from the perspective of TCE, IMP runs the risk of throwing away the baby with the bathwater. Doubtless in present conditions of turbulence, firms require interactions in networks, with trust forming an important dimension in such relations. But there are risks as well: trust is not unbounded; it cannot be taken for granted, and it may break down.

TCE has contributed greatly by specifying rigorously what the nature and extent of risk in transactions are: if there is opportunism and if bounded rationality makes it impossible to foresee it and to foreclose its undesirable consequences, then one runs the risk of loss of investments to the extent that these are relation specific. Next, TCE has supplied indications on how to construct schemes for 'governing' transactions in such a way that risks are reduced. In bilateral private ordering, these include the use of different guarantees to compensate for one-sided transaction specific investments (cross-ownership of assets, hostages, guaranteed price, volume or period of purchase), and countermeasures to guard against invalid use and expropriation of such guarantees. In infrequent transactions, they include trilateral exchange, with some third party acting as an arbiter. These concepts are of theoretical and practical use, and it is wasteful not to apply them.

Both trust and opportunism are likely to arise in transaction relations, and neither should be ignored.

SELF-INTEREST AND TRUST

Note that TCE does not claim that everyone is opportunistic, but that at least some people are opportunistic at least some of the time; since one does not know who or when, it is wise to take into account the possibility of opportunism. Of course, the perception of opportunism may shift as experience with the transaction partner accrues, and this is neglected by TCE. As a transaction relation develops in time, perceived opportunism may decline, but it may also increase. Slight suspicions of opportunism may escalate, even due to misunderstanding, and this may lead to a breakdown of the relation.

While opportunism and trustworthiness seem opposites, trustworthiness may well be a form of calculated long-term self-interest. If many people are untrustworthy, to be trustworthy makes one an attractive partner.[4] Then it pays visibly to forego short-term advantages from opportunism, and thereby build a reputation for trustworthiness. Of course, there are limits to such trustworthiness: when at some point in the future opportunism becomes so tempting as to provide ample recompense for opportunities foregone in the past (in a 'golden opportunity'), opportunism may rear its head after all. Also, there may be weakness of the will: even though one knows that it would be better to forego yet another opportunity for opportunism (in view of investments in reputation in the past and expected benefits from a continued reputation in the future), one may simply succumb to the lure of short-term gain. This indicates that reputation may have its limits of reliability, but it is a valid principle nevertheless.

Another way in which trustworthiness may be related to self-interest is when it springs from fear of retaliation. This can arise, in terms of TCE, when there are relation specific investments on both sides of the relation. Mutual adaptation (in knowledge, technical standards, procedures for planning, administration and communication, social relations and so on) may be seen as wholly or partly transaction specific investments that contribute to mutual lockin.

Of course, trustworthiness may go beyond any self-interest. It may be based on an emotion of friendship or a socially or institutionally ingrained morality which detaches it from self-interest in the short and longer term. Even here, however, the question arises whether there is not some bound to it. Is trustworthiness ever boundless, regardless of its penalty or opportunity cost? In any case, friendship takes time to develop and the degree to which morality is ingrained takes time to discover. This is unless membership of some social group can serve as a reliable indicator of friendship or ingrained morality of trustworthiness, such as membership of one's church community, masonic lodge, school, and so on.

The need for safeguards against opportunism, in case of relation specific investments, is thus likely to depend on the duration of the relation and membership of social groups. It is possible that relations start with low risk transactions, involving modest transaction specific investments. If experience with this slight risk is encouraging, as a result of this and indeed other forms of bonding (including social bonding), expectation of opportunism may be reduced. This may provide the basis for more, and more transaction specific, investments. In this way a virtuous circle of mutual adaptation can come into operation. Here, the emergence of trust is reconstructed partly in terms of transaction cost thinking (transaction specific assets, lockin), and partly in terms outside of TCE, such as social bonding.

Summing up: while TCE lacks dimensions of competence building and trust, it yields useful insights into the conditions, nature and extent of risk in transactions, and ways to guard against such risk. Furthermore, it can contribute to an understanding of how trust may emerge from transactions to contribute to an ongoing relation.

TRANSACTIONS AND INSTITUTIONS

Transaction cost theory is also useful for an understanding of institutions. North (1990) has argued that institutions can be explained as serving to reduce transaction costs, because in an institutional vacuum transaction costs would be too high; that is, they could not be overcome in exchange extending beyond the social bounds and bonds of small communities. Without institutions, transactions would be severely constricted, and hence division of labour and thus prosperity would be limited.[5]

Institutions include physical infrastructure, political structure, legal systems (concerning property rights, contract, liability, advertising, etc.), financial institutions (such as a stable, convertible currency, a two-tier banking system, stock exchange, etc.), technical standards as well as professional and more general moral standards (concerning honesty, humanity, justice, fair play, etc.).

If we view networks as institutions, IMP can perhaps be seen as tying into this way of thinking. Networks serve to develop, contain and protect institutional measures to reduce transaction costs. These include a common language, technical standards, standards of administration, planning, communication, invoicing, payment, but also rules of 'ordinary procedure', 'fair play' and 'common culture'.

Again the question is: might it not strengthen the IMP perspective to pursue this line of thought? But that would imply the incorporation, rather than the rejection, of a transaction cost perspective.

If both TCE and IMP yield useful insights, let us try to construe a unified theory which contains the strengths but eliminates the weaknesses of both. Beneath the surface, the debate is really one between two very different theories of knowledge which remain implicit. It is high time to eliminate the blind spots by bringing this to the surface, so that the debate can focus on where the real issues lie.

FROM CORRESPONDENCE TO COHERENCE[6]

As recognised also by others (Groenewegen, 1989; Hodgson, 1988), transaction cost theory, and neoclassical economics in general, is implicitly based on an old-fashioned epistemology which is increasingly seen to be untenable. The basic view is one of preferences, knowledge, technology and endowments as 'underlying realities'.[7] These are assumed to be exogenous and given. As a result, economics is concerned with the construction of equilibrium in the Pareto sense: allocation of resources so that no one's satisfaction can be improved without reducing someone else's. That is seen as both a normative benchmark and an actual situation (in Walrasian economics); alternatively, it is a horizon to which economic forces tend (in Austrian economics).

Whether economists realise it or not, this view derives from the philosophical perspective of metaphysical realism: there are underlying realities there to be perceived equally by all. But this notion, which represents a strong tradition in Western thought from Plato through to Descartes, is now seen to be illusory.[8]

As goes far beyond the scope of this chapter to fully unravel the issue, we have to be brief and blunt. The notion of underlying realities as objective, identifiable entities makes sense only if we assume that we can step outside of our knowledge to contemplate them. This does not make sense. Rather, as effectively expressed by Neurath's metaphor that was repeatedly invoked by Quine: we construct and reconstruct our knowledge from within, like a mariner who repairs his boat plank by plank while staying afloat in it.[9] As Kant first recognised, we construct even our most basic perceptions in terms of categories that are part of us, not of what we perceive. When we construct representations of reality, we employ instruments of representation that are not themselves part of the representation: the act of representation escapes itself. Thus even facts are the product of construction, while complete objectiveness is an illusion. The stability of the world, as reconstructed in our perception, is likely to be an illusion as well. If it is meaningful to speak of outside reality, which (in view of our inability to grasp it) is problematic, it is likely to be much more chaotic than we perceive in terms of our reconstructions.

In other words: the positivist programme of anchoring knowledge in hard kernels of reality, in basic observation statements, cannot succeed. Truth as correspondence between elements of knowledge and elements of outside reality is unattainable. Note that it is still reasonable to postulate an outside world that somehow has a causal influence on our learning. The point is that we cannot step out to pick up elements of truth from it and must be modest in our claims to represent it.

Does this imply, then, that we must surrender to relativism; that every statement is as good as any other, and that there is no truth left? NO: although all perception and knowledge are constructed, some propositions are more speculative than others. Although there is no guarantee of truth in an absolute sense of correspondence with reality, the facts that we construe together, in intersubjective discourse and experimentation, are generally more reliable than the theoretical speculation of individuals. As was already recognised by Popper: facts are not things we somehow dig up from rock-bottom truth, but things we can reasonably agree on. The criticism of Popper is that we cannot always do so. When there are radical differences of theoretical perspective, people may lack the basis to agree on relevant facts.[10]

Of the essence here is intersubjective variance in perception and knowledge, based on variance of experience in different contexts. In interaction with their physical and social environment, individuals jointly develop common meanings and individually impose idiosyncratic variations upon them. For this to be possible, meaning must be inherently fuzzy, so that an unorthodox usage of linguistic terms cannot immediately be ruled out. It is by virtue of this peculiar combination of commonality and idiosyncracy that meanings and knowledge can develop.[11]

There is also path-dependence involved, in that knowledge developed now is the basis for developing further knowledge in the future. However, if as a result I personally go way off course, I can correct my errors by checking my path against the paths of others, and by arguing about it. We may also go off course collectively as has happened repeatedly in history. One way of trying to prevent this is to learn from history.

Facts are ill-defined in the sense that to some extent they are 'theory laden' being contingent upon theories underlying measurement or interpretation. Thus there is no clear demarcation between fact and theory or, as Quine argued, between the analytic and the synthetic. To use Quine's metaphor: knowledge is a 'seamless web', which along the periphery impinges on the external world that we can still reasonably postulate. What is accepted as factual or analytic in one context of debate may be the object of criticism in another context. Like the mariner, we repair the boat of our knowledge plank by plank while staying afloat inside it.

Is there still truth? Yes, but in a very different sense from correspondence truth, namely coherence truth. We test the adequacy of some part of knowledge (considered to be more speculative) on the basis of the assumed validity of other parts (considered to be more factual). But these judgements of relative speculativeness and factuality depend on the context at hand. As argued elsewhere (Nooteboom, 1986), plausibility as a criterion of theoretical adequacy is related to the concept of truth as coherence.

ECONOMICS AND SOCIOLOGY

From the present perspective, the underlying realities of equilibrium economics are illusory. There are no meaningful preferences prior to all exchange; no technology prior to learning.

Preferences, and indeed meanings that precede preferences, emerge from exchange, in markets viz. communication. As argued by Dietz (1991, 1992), command economies without markets cannot succeed, not for the mere technical reason that planning is difficult (assuming technology and preferences), but for the much more fundamental reason that without market exchange, preferences are ill-formed, are groping in the dark. Value is not defined. Central planning is inherently and literally worthless.

Knowledge emerges from learning, which takes place in interaction with the physical and social environment. It is by assimilating experience from what works and what does not, from what is accepted in markets and what is not, that innovation can have a source and a direction.

Lacking that source and direction, central planning is thereby inherently static.

To come to an adequate understanding of markets, both preference formation and innovation must be made endogenous. If we accept that for lack of objective 'underlying' realities that are somehow 'out there' for everyone to grasp, then both emerge from intersubjective interaction. Therefore, they are part not only of economics but also of sociology, because that is what sociology studies: intersubjective interaction in the formation of knowledge and institutions. Therefore, to achieve our purpose, economics and sociology must be integrated.

DILEMMA OF THE FIRM

In order to act you must choose; you must focus on a particular purpose and align perceptions and interpretations. This is also what a firm must do if it is to succeed: the firm serves as a focusing device.[12] This implies a principle of organisation which could replace the Coase/Williamson explanation in terms of transaction costs: in the absence of transaction costs, one would still need to integrate people in firms, as a focusing device, in order to achieve specific goals, perceptions and interpretations among all possible ones.

This alignment of purpose, perceptions and interpretations within the firm is always needed to some extent. The emphasis that firms place on being clear about their 'mission', expressed in a simple statement and enhanced by symbolism and other cultural means, is meant to establish the necessary alignment. However, the requisite degree of alignment is not the same in all circumstances. This explains why some management gurus preach both alignment 'of all noses in the same direction' in one sentence and chaos in the next ('all noses in different directions'). The explanation is that it depends on where you are in the development of ideas and products. After an innovation, after its initial success, the need for alignment is greatest in order to consolidate success. Later, when an idea or product has exhausted its potential, towards the saturation level of its life cycle, a realignment is required; when the direction of a new alignment is not clear, prior to innovation, there should be less alignment or noses in different directions. The implication is that there should be different arrangements for a product in different stages of its life cycle, and hence different simultaneous arrangements for an organization with different products in different stages.[13]

The notion of the firm as a focusing device points to a dilemma of the firm. Categories of perception, understanding and evaluation are conditioning in the double sense that they enable but also restrict perception, understanding and evaluation. In other words, you lose out on perceptions, meanings and interpretations. The dilemma is more pertinent now than ever before. In present conditions of markets and technology, firms more than ever have to focus on core activities in order to survive, but also more than ever there is a risk of missing out on the perception and interpretation of novel opportunities and threats. Note that categories of perception, understanding and evaluation are path dependent so that one cannot simply buy into them at a given time. Even taking over firms with the appropriate competence may not work, because that competence may break down in the alignments that come into place in the buying firm.

Now networks can be seen as a solution to this dilemma. Network relations certainly perform the role of maximising total efficiency of production, organisation and transaction, as proposed by TCE. But they also serve as a web of external intelligence to solve the dilemma indicated above, and TCE is blind to this. Direct and indirect network contacts serve as antennae to produce and transmit perceptions, interpretations and evaluations. Not just of 'data' but cognitive productions whose relevance is ensured by the fact that network contacts have been chosen for the complementarity and/or similarity of their activities to those of the focal firm.

This might be called the principle of external economy of learning, which might be added to our repertoire of concepts of internal and external economies of scale and scope. While TCE proposes, as an argument for contracting out, the economy of scale that a specialised producer might achieve, we now add external economy of learning as an additional argument. One could perhaps even suggest that this idea is already implicit in TCE, but that seems to stretch interpretation a bit too far.

INTEGRATING TCE AND IMP

In our attempt to integrate TCE and IMP in a generalised theory of firms and their relations, problems still have to be solved.

In the two theoretical perspectives, boundedness of rationality leads to opposite recommendations concerning outsourcing. According to TCE, bounded rationality is a cause of transaction costs, which discourages for example outsourcing. In IMP, at least as it is reconstructed and perhaps extended here, bounded rationality prompts a requirement for external intelligence, which favours outsourcing. The solution of this paradox is that two different aspects of bounded rationality are referred to. In the former, the issue is lack or asymmetry of information concerning intentions of transaction partners and future contingencies that might affect the terms of the transaction. In the second, the issue is the impossibility or undesirability (in view of the need to focus on core activities) to produce all relevant perceptions, interpretations and evaluations concerning opportunities and threats outside of the transaction. I propose that both issues are relevant.

A second paradox concerns the desirability of lockin or bonding as a result of embeddedness in the transaction relation due to relation specific investments. These could include mutual knowledge about contacts, formal and informal organisation, technology, procedures, norms and rules; common language; organisational linkages in hardware or software; social ties and friendship. According to TCE these contribute to lockin and hence to transaction costs, and are therefore undesirable. According to IMP they contribute to bonding and therefore trust, and are thus desirable. Again both views are correct and useful. The IMP view is correct, even from the perspective of TCE, in that to the extent that bonding contributes to symmetry of lockin, it makes for partial (but not complete) mutual assurance against opportunism.[14] In addition to that, the bonding may create trustworthiness that goes beyond self-interest. The TCE view is correct in that one should be aware that bonding creates switching costs which one may regret in case of an unforeseen need to switch.

The different views are reconciled in the diagram in Figure 1.2 which represents an extension with respect to TCE, and could be built into IMP.[15] Figure 1.2 does not pretens to represent a full causal web of networks, but shows how parts of TCE and IMP can be brought together.

In particular, we see how embeddedness (bonding) increases dependency, which contributes to 'risk of dependence' (which indicates the possible negative results), while at the same time it may decrease opportunism. Thus the net effect is, in principle, ambiguous. It depends on the type of bonding, its symmetry and the level of the perceived threat of opportunism. Safeguards already in place reduce risk of dependence (that is why they were instituted). The model implies a sequence of periods or transactions; within each period, the question can be raised whether further safeguards are required or not. Of course the fact that safeguards are required need not imply that they will be installed. As experience accrues, perceived opportunism may decline. Its likelihood may also depend on social groupings and ties.

Figure 1.2 An extended causal scheme

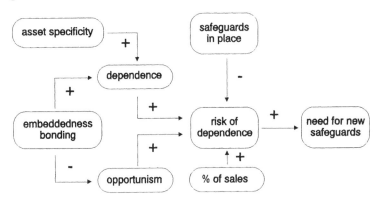

CONCLUSION

In the race for innovation and markets, firms need relations with other firms. Not only to benefit from specialisation in the narrow sense in which economies of scale are realised, but because, from different histories in different contexts of markets and technology, different firms have different competences in skills and cognition. Those capabilities cannot be adopted or transferred instantaneously, so that to benefit from them one must entertain a more or less lasting relationship with the firm involved.

Since perceptions, preferences and knowledge develop in the course of exchange, many factors (including productive potential of the relation, perceptions of opportunism, bonds due to mutually specific investments and other institutions that reduce transaction costs) develop through time. This can explain the occurrence of transaction specific investments without visible safeguards of the type prescribed by TCE.[16] However, mistrust and opportunism may also escalate to destroy a relation.

This does not invalidate all of TCE. The notions of transaction specificity, potential opportunism and lockin are still useful in order to be precise about risks and trust and to contribute to an understanding of how risks may be reduced and how trust may emerge in an exchange relation.

In a sense, the problem with TCE is that it does not carry the issue of bounded rationality far enough into a new theory of knowledge without 'underlying realities'. We have shown that when this is done, interfirm relations assume a new dimension that is also found in the IMP framework. The price we have to pay is the recognition that what we are doing here is integrating sociology with economics, and that this is inevitable.

Let us then get on with it.[17]

NOTES

1. For an application in the Netherlands, see Biemans (1989).
2. At least if by sociology one means the symbolic interaction stream of sociology. The rational choice stream of sociology is much easier to reconcile with economics, because it imports much of the economic perspective into sociology.
3. The final purpose of this programme will certainly not be reached in this chapter, but an attempt at progress is made.
4. Cf. Frank (1988).
5. For a consideration of effects of scale in transaction costs, see Nooteboom (1992a), and for the implications for institutions enabling the operation of small business, see Nooteboom (1992b).
6. For a more extensive discussion, see Nooteboom (1986).
7. Cf. Dietz (1992).
8. As a result of a line of philosophical thought running from Kant via Hegel, Nietzsche, Freud and Heidegger to a line in Anglo-Saxon and a more or less parallel line in French thought. In Anglo-Saxon thought: Peirce, Quine, Wittgenstein, Goodman, Rorty. In French thought: de Saussure, Bachelard, Merleau-Ponty and the 'postmodernists': Foucault, Lyotard, Derrida, Deleuze, *et al.*
9. The metaphor illustrates the view, in Quine (1951), of knowledge as a 'seamless web' of both theory and observation. See the related discussion of the concept of plausibility in Nooteboom (1986).
10. Cf. Kuhn (1962).
11. For a study of the theory of language of Ferdinand de Saussure, to investigate this issue, and its application to a theory of markets and innovation, see Nooteboom (1992c).
12. This is close to the notion of 'enactment' proposed by Weick (1979).
13. Similar ideas were expressed by Weick (1982). For further discussion based on a stage theory of learning, development and innovation, see Nooteboom (1989). For an application to transaction cost theory, see Nooteboom (1992c).
14. Not complete, because the partner may turn out to be vindictive or emotional, in harming himself in spite of his own loss, out of a greater desire to harm the partner.
15. For an attempt to develop an empirical test of TCE against an extended framework, see Berger, Noorderhaven, Nooteboom and Pennink (1993).
16. Cf. Semlinger (1991).
17. For attempts at progress in making transaction cost theory dynamic, see Nooteboom (1992c), and in embedding transactions in time, space, networks and sociality, see Berger, Noorderhaven, Nooteboom and Pennink (1993).

REFERENCES

Berger, J., N.G. Noorderhaven, B. Nooteboom and B.J. Pennink (1993), 'Understanding the Subcontracting Relationship; The Limitations of Transaction Cost Economics', in J. Child, M. Crozier, R. Mayntz *et al.* (eds.), *Societal Change Between Market and Organization*. Frankfurt: Campus/Westview, in press.

Biemans, W.G. (1989), *Developing Innovations Within Networks*, Ph D. Thesis. Eindhoven, the Netherlands.

Coase, R.H. (1937), 'The Nature of the Firm', *Economica*, 4, 386-405.

Dietz, R. (1991), *From Command to Market Economies - An Exchange Theoretical View*, paper presented at EAEPE conference, Vienna.

Dietz, R. (1992), *Tausch und Rationalität von Wirtschaftssystemen - Ein Beitrag zur Begrundung eines systemtheoretischen Paradigmas*. The Vienna Institute for Comparative Economic Studies.

Frank, R.H. (1988), *Emotions Within Reason, The Strategic Role of the Emotions*. New York: Norton.

Groenewegen, J. (1989), 'De transaktiekosten nader bezien', *Tijdschrift voor Politieke Economie*, 12 (4), 51-76.

Håkansson, H. (ed.) (1982), *International Marketing and Purchasing of Industrial Goods - An Interaction Approach*. Chichester: Wiley.

Håkansson, H. (ed.) (1987), *Industrial Technological Development: A Network Approach*. London: Croom Helm.

Hodgson, G.M. (1988), *Economics and Institutions*. Cambridge: Polity Press.

Johanson, J. and L.G. Mattson (1985), 'Marketing Investments and Market Investments in Industrial Networks', *International Journal of Research in Marketing*, 2, 185-195.

Johanson, J. and L.G. Mattson (1987), *Interorganisational Relations in Industrial Systems - A Network Approach Compared with the Transaction Cost Approach*, University of Uppsala.

Kuhn, T.S. (1962), *The Structure of Scientific Revolutions*. Chicago: Chicago University Press.

Nooteboom, B. (1986), 'Plausibility in Economics', *Economics and Philosophy*, 2, 197-224.

Nooteboom, B. (1989), 'Paradox, Identity and Change in Management', *Human Systems Management*, 8, 291-300.

Nooteboom, B. (1992a), *Small Business, Institutions and Economic Systems*, paper presented at EAEPE conference, Paris.

Nooteboom, B. (1992b), 'Towards a Dynamic Theory of Transactions', *Journal of Evolutionary Economics*, 2, 281-299.

Nooteboom, B. (1992c), 'Agent, Context and Innovation: A Saussurian View of Markets' in: W. Blaas and J. Foster (ed.), *Mixed Economies in Europe: An Evolutionary Perspective on their Emergence, Transition and Regulation*. Aldershot: Edward Elgar.

Nooteboom, B. (1993), 'Firms Size Effects on Transaction Costs', *Small Business Economics*, in press.

North, D.C. (1990), *Institutions, Institutional Change and Economic Performance*, Cambridge: Cambridge University Press.

Quine, W.V.O. (1951), 'Two Dogmas of Empiricism', *The Philosophical Review*, 60, 20-43

Semlinger, K. (1991), *Innovation, Cooperation and Strategic Contracting*, paper presented at International Colloquium on Management of Technology, Paris.

Weick, K.E. (1979), *The Social Psychology of Organizations*. Reading Mass: Addison Wesley.

Weick, K.E. (1982), 'Management of Organizational Change Among Loosely Coupled Elements', in: P.S. Goodman *et al.* (eds.), *Change in Organizations: New Perspectives in Theory, Research, and Practice*. San Francisco: Jossey-Bass.

Williamson, O.E. (1975), *Markets and Hierarchies: Analysis and Antitrust Implications*. New York: The Free Press.

Williamson, O.E. (1985), *The Economic Institutions of Capitalism; Firms, Markets, Relational Contracting*. New York: The Free Press.

2. Facts, Theory and the Pricing Foundation of Post Keynesian Price Theory

Fred Lee

INTRODUCTION

Surveys of Post Keynesian economics have largely concentrated on the contributions of specific individuals and approaches. Consequently when the net is cast widely, Post Keynesian economics includes strands of classical political economy, Marxism, Sraffian economics, Institutionalism, and Keynesian economics; on the other hand, if the net is drawn more narrowly, then we have Post Keynesian economics vs Sraffian economics vs Kaleckian economics. This, of course, leaves Post Keynesian economics largely undefined, especially to the outsider, and susceptible to neoclassical ideas. There have also been attempts to define a theoretical core in terms of Keynes and classical political economy so as to give it some coherence. But such endeavours have, ironically, actually undermined the name of Post Keynesian economics; for if Sraffa, Marx and Keynes are thought to provide the core of the Post Keynesian research programme, then Post Classical economics would seem the more appropriate nomenclature. However, even these attempts at establishing a theoretical core for Post Keynesian economics would fail if the microfoundations of its research programme were not based entirely on Keynes, Sraffa or Marx.

In most surveys of Post Keynesian economics, attention is given to its microfoundations; however, the discussion is usually restricted to the Kaleckian tradition as extended and developed, say, by J. Steindl, P. Sylos-Labini, S. Weintraub and A.S. Eichner, or to the Sraffian approach to prices. This restricted perception of microeconomics follows from the strongly held view that macroeconomics determines its own microfoundations. Because of this, Post Keynesians have devoted little energy towards articulating a consistent and realistic microfoundation and largely ignored 'micro' themes and issues, such as the business enterprise, pricing, the organisation of markets, the nature of competitive activities, coordination of economic activity, and innovation and technical change. As a result, there exists no well-grounded cohesive body of economic analysis that could be referred to as Post Keynesian microeconomics. Rather the microeconomics accepted and utilised by Post Keynesians tends to be rather idiosyncratic, although there are biases towards particular tools, concepts and approaches. No better example of this exists than in the area of pricing by business enterprises in industrial, wholesale and retail markets.

When considering macroeconomic or microeconomic issues, Post Keynesians have utilised three distinct pricing or price-setting procedures in their writings: mark-up, normal cost, and target rate of return pricing procedures; however, a majority of them prefer Kaleckian or Weintraubian mark-up pricing procedures based on constant average direct costs. Yet the evidence is clear that all three pricing procedures are widely used by business enterprises in industrial market economies, although some evidence suggests that enterprise size (as measured by sales) and degree of diversification play an important role in determining the choice of pricing procedure. Moreover, the empirical evidence (see Lee, 1986) on average direct costs and average direct labour costs clearly shows that they are, in general, not constant. Consequently, in emphasising a single pricing procedure in conjunction with constant average direct costs in their research, Post Keynesians have clearly violated economic reality. Whether this violation is 'significant' or not with respect to the research being conducted is not known since no Post Keynesian has even paused to contemplate the question, much less devise a means to answer it.

Compounding the above ignorance is the habit of Post Keynesians to employ the chosen pricing procedure as a stylised fact without realising that it has a number of inherent and associated properties which often makes it inconsistent with the research being done. This habit thrives because Post Keynesians are largely unaware of the vast number of empirical investigations on or related to pricing procedures and to their place in the strategic activities of the business enterprise. The purpose of this chapter is to offer an empirically grounded pricing model that will provide the foundation on which a coherent and realistic price theory can be developed. This will be done in a piecemeal fashion. In particular, the first two sections will be devoted to two facets of pricing and the business enterprise: (1) the business enterprise's pricing equation, and (2) pricing, the business enterprise and the market. Each will be examined empirically and, at times, theoretically, with special attention being paid to the implications for the

Kaleckian, Weintraubian and Sraffian contributions to Post Keynesian price theory. The third section of this chapter will delineate an empirically grounded pricing model whose properties make it incompatible with the Kaleckian, Weintraubian and Sraffian-inspired Post Keynesian pricing models. The chapter will conclude that this model, while indebted to a limited extent to the above Post Keynesian theoretical traditions, cannot be identified as Post Keynesian *per se* or as being based solely on the works of Marx, Keynes and Sraffa. This implies, it will be argued, that the price theory for which the empirically grounded pricing model is a foundation must have a different name.

SOME CONCEPTS

Before starting, the differences between costing procedures, pricing procedures and prices need to be delineated in order to facilitate the subsequent discussion. *Costing* refers to the procedures a business enterprise employs to determine the costs that will be used in setting the selling price of a good before actual production takes place and hence before the actual costs of production are known. The procedures are based on an estimated, normal or standard volume of output or capacity utilisation and can range from determining estimated average direct costs to determining the normal or standard average total costs which consist of normal average direct costs, average shop expenses[1] and average firm expenses[2], with average shop and firm expenses together being the enterprise's average overhead costs. *Pricing* refers to the procedures the business enterprise uses to set the price of a good before it is produced and placed on the market. That is, starting with the costs determined by its costing procedures, the business enterprise then adds a costing margin to costs or marks up the costs to set the price. Finally, *the price* is the enterprise's selling price which is determined via its pricing procedures and therefore is set before production and exchange take place. Besides the distinctions made above, there exist two general types of costing procedures: estimated costing and standard costing. In the former, costs are determined by methods that range from a perfunctory guess to a very careful computation based upon past experience; in either case, past costs are used as the basis to determine the costs of a good that will be produced in the future. In the latter, costs are determined by a process of scientific fact-finding which utilises both past experience and controlled experiments and occurs in advance of production. However, in spite of the differences, both estimated and standard costing arrive at the costs of producing a good that will be used in setting the price in the same way. Hence in the following discussion reference will only be made to costing, unless otherwise noted.

The activities of costing and pricing are carried out within the business enterprise by an individual, such as its owner, or by a committee made up of business administrators or managers drawn from different departments and levels of management. In either case, costing and pricing are activities which are controlled by the administrators (see Appendix 2.1, nos. 7, 12, 14, 17 and Appendix 2.2, nos. 1, 19, 21, 22, 28, 31, 32, 33, 40, 44, 50, 55, 63, 64; also see Nourse and Drury, 1938; Nourse, 1944; Gordon, 1945; Cassady, 1954; and Chandler, 1962 and 1977). Consequently, the kind of costing and pricing procedures used within the business enterprise, including how depreciation and normal output or capacity utilisation are calculated, are administratively determined. Moreover, the prices thus determined are dictated to the market; for example business enterprises utilise costing and pricing procedures as a method through which they can impose their prices on the market.

The administratively-determined pricing procedures that will be the focal point of this chapter include mark-up, normal cost, and target rate of return pricing. *Mark-up pricing procedures* consist of either marking up average direct labour costs based on normal or estimated output to set the price, with the mark-up being sufficient to cover material costs (if any), shop and firm expenses (that is overhead costs), and produce a profit; or it can consist of marking up average direct costs based on normal or estimated output to set the price, with the mark-up being sufficient to cover shop and firm expenses and produce a profit. *Normal cost pricing procedures* consist of marking up average direct costs based on normal output to cover shop expenses, which gives normal average factory costs, then marking up these to cover firm expenses, which gives normal average total costs, and then marking up the latter to set the price, with the mark-up producing a desired margin for profit. Finally *target rate of return pricing procedures* consist of marking up standard average total costs (which include shop and firm expenses) by a certain per cent that will generate a volume of profits at standard capacity utilisation; this will produce a specific rate of return with respect to the value of the enterprise's capital assets. The above pricing procedures can be delineated in the following manner:

labour based mark-up pricing: $[W][1 + s] = \text{price}$
labour and material-based
    mark-up pricing: $[NADC][1 + k] = \text{price}$
normal cost pricing: $[(NADC)(1 + g)][1 + h][1 + r] = \text{price}$
                            $[(NAFC)(1 + h)][1 + r] = \text{price}$

$$[NATC][1 + r] = price$$

target rate of return pricing: $[SATC][1 + t] = price$

where: W is average direct labour costs based on normal output;
   NADC is normal average direct costs;
   NAFC is normal average factory costs;
   NATC is normal average total costs;
   SATC is standard average total costs;
   s   is the mark-up for material costs, overhead costs and profits;
   k   is the mark-up for overhead costs and profits;
   g   is the mark-up for shop expenses;
   h   is the mark-up for firm expenses;
   r   is the mark-up for profit; and
   t   is the mark-up for profit which will produce the target rate of return with respect to the value of the enterprise's capital assets.

It is particularly important to note that for normal cost and target rate of return pricing procedures, business enterprises first identify and quantify their shop and firm expenses, which are generally joint costs, and then decide on how they will be allocated to their various products. The allocating procedures used range from applying a predetermined mark-up on direct labour costs, on direct material costs (or on both) to using machine hours. In all cases, the methods used are based on past experience and scientific fact-finding. Consequently, enterprises use normal cost and target rate of return pricing procedures to arrive at a product's average total cost on which they then apply a mark-up for profit to set the price. Therefore, it is conceptually inappropriate to reduce normal cost or target rate of return pricing procedures to a mark-up pricing procedure, since the latter is only used by enterprises who cannot (or do not) identify, quantify and allocate their overhead costs among their products and who cannot (or do not) separate costs from profits. Hence, the separate mark-up, normal cost and target rate of return procedures will be maintained throughout this chapter.

BUSINESS ENTERPRISE'S PRICING EQUATION

Mark-up, normal cost and target rate of return pricing procedures have been used by large and small business enterprises under various competitive conditions since before the 1930s, as evidenced by the pricing studies summarised in Appendix 2.2. It is also clear from the costing and pricing studies that normal cost and target rate of return pricing are the two procedures most used by business enterprises. For example, in their study of cost accounting in American industry, Black and Eversole (Appendix

2.1, no. 5) found that of the 20,282 enterprises which used a recognisable cost system to determine their costs, nearly 90 per cent of them could calculate their average factory costs and nearly 80 per cent their average total costs. It can then be argued (see Simon *et al.*, 1954 and Chandler, 1962) that the enterprises would use the developed cost base when engaging in costing and pricing. The costing studies (Appendix 2.1 nos. 4, 6-8, 11-16, 18-21, 23) do in fact support this argument, while the costing-pricing study by Govindarajan and Anthony (Appendix 2.1 no. 10) cements it. More significantly, only twenty of the fifty-eight pricing studies in Appendix 2.2 report the use of mark-up pricing (see Table 2.1), and of these studies only two reported the existence of labour-based mark-up pricing, while the costing studies (see Appendix 2.1), which reported on the use of direct and variable costing, show that only 21 per cent of the 1335 enterprises surveyed utilised the procedures. Finally, the costing and pricing studies also indicated that many of the enterprises which utilised mark-up pricing procedures restricted their usage to secondary pricing decisions and special cases, such as pricing by products, subcontracting, disposing of obsolete and outdated production, and determining price floors in extreme price-cutting situations (see Appendix 2.1. nos. 8, 11, 12, 23; and Appendix 2.2, nos. 31, 44, 57, 60, 64).

Table 2.1   Distribution of pricing procedures reported in Appendix 2.2

	LBMUP	LMBMUP	NCP	TRRP
number of studies reporting the pricing procedure	2	20	46	16

LBMUP	— labour based mark-up pricing
LMBMUP	— labour and material-based mark-up pricing
NCP	— normal cost pricing
TRRP	— target rate of return pricing

Regarding the costing procedures themselves, we find that the specific figure for normal capacity or estimated production is administratively determined and that its determinants range from anticipated sales for the period under review, anticipated sales for a period of years into the future and average sales experience for a number of past years, to the practical capacity of the enterprise (see Appendix 2.1, nos. 3, 12, 20, 23; and Appendix 2.2, nos. 1, 5, 6, 7, 8, 10, 13, 14, 16, 17, 22, 33, 43). As for the depreciation component in shop and firm expenses, business enterprises have used (see for instance Hodgkins, 1979 and Vangermeersch, 1979) and continue to use both historical costs for valuing plant and equipment for depreciation purposes and the straight line or declining charges methods for calculating the depreciation allowance which appears in the costing calculations (see Appendix 2.1, nos. 2, 10, 12, 13, 14, 16, 17, 20, 22, 23; and Appendix 2.2, nos. 6, 16, 23, 33). Moreover the tax codes in the United States, Germany and France stipulate that business enterprises must use historical costs for valuing plant and equipment, while the tax code in the United Kingdom states that enterprises can use either historical or current costs, although most use historical costs for valuing plant and equipment (Appendix 2.1, no. 22 and Appendix 2.2, no. 16; and Nobes, 1985). Finally, none of the costing procedures delineated in the costing and pricing studies included a component for profit.

One implication that can be drawn from the above evidence is that in a capitalist economy, such as found in the United States, the United Kingdom, Denmark, Australia and Germany, business enterprises use a variety of costing and pricing procedures; therefore any theoretical analysis or empirical investigation of a capitalist economy which is based on a single pricing procedure is inconsistent with economic reality. Moreover, the overwhelming usage of normal cost and target rate of return pricing procedures by business enterprises for most (and always primary) pricing decisions clearly implies that those Kaleckian studies which utilise labour and material-based mark-up pricing cannot claim to have anything more than minority status, and that the Weintraubian studies relying on labour-based mark-up pricing are simply 'false' in that they are not dealing with economic reality at all. Finally, those studies, for example Kregel (1975), Harcourt and Kenyon (1976), Ong (1981), Dutt (1988) and Sawyer (1990), which combine mark-up pricing, large business enterprises and growth are empirically and theoretically misleading in that mark-up pricing is more likely to be associated with small enterprises (of the ten pricing studies involving small enterprises and delineating pricing procedures, nine of them reported the use of mark-up pricing) whose goals and objectives are survival, satisfactory profits and customer satisfaction (see Appendix 2.2, nos. 11, 25, 26, 27, 29, 36, 39, 40, 48).

A second implication to be drawn is that, since the costs used for pricing are based on estimated production or normal capacity, the question of the shape of the average direct cost curve is immaterial for pricing purposes. Consequently, since actual average direct, factory and total costs can differ from their costed counterparts when actual production or capacity utilisation differs from what was estimated or taken as normal, it is not surprising, first, that the actual mark-ups for profit (k, r and t) can differ from the ones used to set the price or, second, that the actual rate of return differs from the targeted rate of return.

A third implication regarding the different methods by which business enterprises determine normal output or capacity utilisation is that the various Sraffian definitions, such as a cost minimising rate of utilisation (Kurz, 1986 and 1990) or the expected utilisation of a new plant that has been or might be installed (Ciccone, 1987 and 1990), are either inconsistent or only partially congruent with the facts. Furthermore, since the figure for normal output or estimated production is administratively determined, it is possible for business enterprises to alter it over the business cycle, resulting in the costed average factory or average total costs increasing in the downturn and decreasing in the upturn. If the mark-ups remain constant, then enterprises would be setting counter-cyclical or 'perverse' prices which are incompatible with the cross-dual price models of classical political economy (Dumenil and Levy, 1991; Arena, 1990; Boggio, 1992; Blair, 1974; and Means, 1983).[3]

A fourth implication is that, given the manner in which business enterprises deal with depreciation, the Sraffian treatment of depreciation is inconsistent with economic reality since business enterprises have not and do not treat their fixed capital as a joint product and therefore do not value it at market prices when calculating depreciation for costing and pricing purposes. Thus, the theoretical studies which utilise the Sraffian approach to depreciation are, as a result, in violation of economic reality, not to mention in violation of the law as symbolised by the tax code. Moreover, because nearly all business enterprises value their fixed capital assets at historical costs, the target rate of return (whether it be reasonable or fair, high or low) which is utilised in setting prices is simply not the same as the rate of profit found in Marxian and Sraffian studies. Hence to equate the two and then argue that business enterprises are directly setting long period prices, as e.g. Clifton (1983) and Semmler (1984) do, is nonsensical.

The final implication is that, since none of the costing procedures delineated in the costing and pricing studies included a component for profit, it is clear that business enterprises have not and do not consider profits as part of costs. Consequently, the typical statement made by Sraffians and Marxists that prices equal their costs of production in long period positions has no correspondence with the concepts of costs and prices as used by business people. Without this link many of the theoretical categories of Sraffians and Marxists can be seen to refer to a purely fictitious world, a world that has no room for actual business enterprises and their costing and pricing procedures.

PRICING, THE BUSINESS ENTERPRISE AND THE MARKET

Considerable research (by Carlton, Kashyap and Blinder (see Appendix 2.3, Means, 1939, and Riley, 1958) has established that, in the United States, prices of most industrial and retail goods remain unchanged for extended periods of time and for many sequential transactions. In addition, thirty-four of the studies in Appendix 2.2 reveal that enterprises which used mark-up, normal cost and target rate of return pricing procedures adopted policies designed to maintain prices for the selling season and in face of fluctuations in sales. Finally, Blinder in his study (see Appendix 2.3) noted that the enterprises thought that the use of cost-based or normal cost pricing procedures was an important factor in explaining infrequent price changes. Thus, it can be concluded that an essential facet of mark-up, normal cost and target rate of return pricing procedures is that enterprises use them to set prices that they intend to maintain for periods of time and many sequential transactions. Conversely, it can also be concluded that prices of products which change infrequently have been set by enterprises using the above pricing procedures. Consequently, it can generally be concluded that a significant proportion of industrial and consumer products in a capitalist economy have prices which are based on mark-up, normal cost and target rate of return pricing procedures.

One feature of stable, cost-based prices is that they are determined before transactions take place and are administered to the market, hence their name of administered prices. A second feature of administered prices is the absence of any determinant inverse price-sales relationship facing the individual business enterprise or the market as a whole. Where reported (see Appendix 2.2, nos. 1, 5, 6, 10, 11, 14, 16, 19, 21, 24, 26, 30, 31, 34, 36, 40, 41, 48, 55, 64), business enterprises stated that variations in their prices within practical limits, given the prices of their competitors, produced virtually no change in their sales and that variations in the market price, especially downward, produced little if any changes in market sales in the short term. Moreover, when the price decrease has been significant enough to result in a non-insignificant upturn in sales, the impact on profits has been so serious as to pursuade enterprises not to try the experiment again (for example, Bell, 1960). The absence of any significant market price-sales relationship in the short term has also been noted in various industry studies (for example, Cassady, 1954). Consequently, business enterprises do not utilise an inverse price-sales relationship when making pricing decisions; nor do they set their prices to achieve a specific volume of sales. Instead the prices they set are maintained despite fluctuations in sales volumes over time.[4] In fact, enterprises believe that sales are almost entirely a function of buyer income, level of aggregate economic activity, government demand for armaments, population growth, product design, and perhaps advertising (see Appendix 2.2, nos. 1, 5, 19, 41, 58).

The third feature of administered prices is that they change over time. As the evidence indicates, business enterprises maintain pricing periods of three months to a year (see Appendix 2.2, nos. 5, 6, 9, 19, 21, 22, 24, 30, 33, 40, 42, 43, 45, 52, 55, 61) in which their administered prices remain unchanged; then, at the end of the period, they decide on whether to alter them. The factors which are most important to the enterprises in this regard are changes in labour and material costs (see Appendix 2.2, nos. 4, 5, 6, 7, 13, 19, 21, 22, 24, 26, 28, 29, 30, 31, 34, 35, 37, 39, 40, 41, 43, 44, 46, 47, 64), changes in the mark-up for profit (see Appendix 2.2, nos. 1, 4, 6, 25, 28, 31, 43, 44), and changes in normal output or capacity utilisation that are based on expected future sales (see Appendix 2.1, nos. 12, 20; and Appendix 2.2, nos. 5, 6, 7, 8, 10, 14, 16, 17, 33, 43).[5] Factors prompting the enterprises to alter their mark-ups for profit include short-term and long-term competitive pressures (see Appendix 2.2, nos. 4, 6, 23, 30, 33, 39, 40, 43, 44, 62), the stage at which the product has reached in its life cycle (see Appendix 2.2, nos. 31, 40, 44, 62), and the need for profit (see Appendix 2.2, nos. 43, 46, 62). Consequently, administered prices can change from one pricing period to the next in any direction, irrespective of the state of the business cycle. However, evidence does suggest that within short periods of time (such as two-year intervals), changes in costs will dominate price changes, whereas over longer periods of time changes in the mark-up will play a more important role.

The final feature of administered prices which is of interest is its role in the reproduction of the business enterprise. As argued elsewhere (see Lee, 1985 and 1990-91), the business enterprise uses cost-based pricing procedures to set prices that will enable it to engage in sequential acts of production over time and thereby reproduce itself and grow. More specifically, because the market conditions facing the enterprise's many products are not uniform and change over time, its price administrators necessarily utilise a variety of multi-temporal, open-ended pricing strategies designed to achieve time specific and temporally undefined goals. This compendium of pricing strategies is known as the enterprise's pricing policy, the prices which it administers to the various markets being based on one or more of these strategies. Thus the administered prices of a business enterprise are strategic prices whose common and overriding goals are often reproduction and growth, but there could be others as well (see Appendix 2.1, nos. 23; and Appendix 2.2, nos. 1, 4, 18, 19, 22, 23, 24, 25, 27, 31, 32, 33, 37, 39, 40, 41, 44, 50, 53, 54, 55, 60, 62, 63, 64).

FACTS, THEORY AND AN EMPIRICALLY GROUNDED POST KEYNESIAN PRICING MODEL

The discussion of the previous sections focused on the pricing procedures and pricing equation of the individual enterprise, both in terms of themselves and their connection with the market. To go beyond the isolated pricing equation to a general model of market pricing equations, it is necessary, first, to develop the individual market pricing equation and state how the market price is established and, second, to integrate the individual market pricing equation into a general system or model of interdependent market pricing equations. The motivation for taking these steps is that the pricing model which is to be the foundation of Post Keynesian price theory must be sufficiently broad so that the ensuing theory of prices can claim general relevance and appropriateness.

Most products are produced and supplied to the market by more than a single business enterprise. Consequently, coordination is required among the enterprises if destructive price competition is to be avoided and an acceptable, single market price is to be established. Therefore, business enterprises have turned to organising secondary bureaucratic organisations in the guise of either market organisations (such as trade associations, cartels, open price associations and price leadership organisations), or, if the purely market organisations fail in their tasks, quasi- or purely government organisations, legal decrees and laws. In cases where a trade association or cartel is involved in fixing the market price, the price administrators may take the average total costs of the member enterprises with the lowest costs adjusted for share of market sales; or they may take an average of costs of all their member enterprises. In either case, a mark-up for profit is applied to the costing equation to set the market price. On the other hand, they may adopt the pricing equation and price of the lowest cost enterprise as the market pricing equation and market price. Finally, a trade association may simply specify the costing and pricing procedures, but not a particular market price, with the consequence that in some markets, such as the printing and book trades, there will not be a single market price (see Appendix 2.2, nos. 14, 15, 19, 21, 22, 33, 34, 35, 44, 51, 59, 60, 61, 64). As for price leadership, the price leader uses its pricing equation to set the market price, while the price following enterprises accept this and adjust their mark-ups for profit accordingly (see Appendix 2.2, nos. 1, 6, 15, 31, 32, 33, 34, 39, 41, 51, 62). Finally, in the case of government determining the market price, the costing and pricing procedures used are the same as those employed by private business enterprises (see Appendix 2.1, no. 7 and Appendix 2.2, nos. 22, 44; and the Select Committee on National Expenditure, 1941).

As delineated, the market pricing equation based on pricing procedures used by the market price administrators has a number of salient features, the most notable being that it has no one universal specification. That is, given the various ways in which the market price equation is and historically has been specified, it is not empirically valid to claim, for example as Eichner (1991) does, that all market pricing equations in industrial and wholesale markets are simply those of the reigning price leader. Moreover, it is also not legitimate to argue for fictional 'representative firm' market pricing equations since all equations are based on real-life enterprises which may or may not be 'representative' of the enterprises in the market. A second salient feature of the market pricing equation is that it is not an average aggregate of all the individual pricing equations. Consequently, the averaging procedure used by Kalecki (1954) to obtain a general market pricing equation has no empirical support. The third salient feature of the market pricing equation is that it is collectively determined by price administrators within the context of social institutions and legal constraints. Hence, it must be concluded that the market pricing equation and the market price are socially and institutionally determined to achieve socially agreed objectives. The final salient feature of the market pricing equation is that the resulting market price is an administered price.

To move from a single market pricing equation to a model of interdependent market pricing equations, it is necessary first to delineate the material, labour and other inputs that are included in the mark-up, normal cost, and target rate of return pricing equations:

mark-up pricing equation

$$\left[\sum_{i=1}^{n} md_{1i}\, p_i + \sum_{v=1}^{z} ld_{1v}w_v \right]\ [1+k_1] = p_1$$

normal cost pricing equation

$$\left[\sum_{i=1}^{n} md_{1i}\, p_i + \sum_{v=1}^{z} ld_{1v}w_v \right]\ [\,1+g_1\,]\ [\,1+h_1\,]\ [\,1+r_1\,] = p_1$$

normal cost pricing equation

$$\left[\sum_{i=1}^{n} md_{1i}\, p_1 + \sum_{v=1}^{z} ld_{1v}w_v + \sum_{i=n+1}^{a} mo_{1i} + \sum_{v=z+1}^{e} lo_{1v}w_w + d_1 \right]\ [\,1+r_1\,] = p_1$$

target rate of return pricing equation

$$[\sum_{i=1}^{n} md_{1i} \, p_1 + \sum_{v=1}^{z} ld_{1v} \, w_v + \sum_{i=n+1}^{a} mo_{1i} + \sum_{v=z+1}^{e} lo_{1v} \, w_w + d_1 \,] \, [1 + t_1] = p_1$$

where: md_{1i} is the ith normal average direct material pricing coefficient;
ld_{1v} is the vth normal average direct labour pricing coefficient;
mo_{1i} is the ith normal average overhead material pricing coefficient;
lo_{1v} is the vth normal average overhead labour pricing coefficient;
d_1 is the normal average depreciation pricing coefficient;
p_i is the market price of the ith material input;
w_v is the wage rate of the vth labour input; and
p_1 is the market price for good 1.

Assuming the existence of, say, $\underline{f}$ markets whose prices are based on the above pricing equations, it is possible to arrange these equations into a system or model of pricing equations. Aside from the obvious feature of the model - that it is empirically grounded since each of its market pricing equations is based on a 'real world' pricing equation - there are a number of other features which need to be delineated. First, that it is a single product pricing model, even though the underlying structure of production includes much joint production. This is based on the fact that enterprises use single product pricing equations when setting prices. A second feature of the model, which follows from the first, is its incomplete and imprecise correspondence with the underlying model of production. This is due to the fact that many of the market pricing equations do not explicitly include all the material and labour inputs actually used in production, leading to the mismeasurement by the market price-setting administrators of the pricing coefficients *vis-à-vis* the actual production coefficients (which accounts for the existence of variance analysis); to the inability of the pricing administrators actually to determine all the pricing coefficients needed for pricing; and to the clear existence of joint production. The final feature of the model is that depreciation pricing coefficients are in money terms, determined prior to the pricing process and largely by the tax code.

As a whole, the four features produce an empirically grounded pricing model that has properties that make it quite different from the Kaleckian, Weintraubian and Sraffian-inspired Post Keynesian pricing models. One, and possibly the most significant, property of the model is that it does not have a dual relationship between prices and quantities (as typically assumed in Post Keynesian production price models) since the pricing coefficients in the pricing model and the production coefficients in the quantity model are not exactly the same. Therefore, it is theoretically conceivable that market prices may not carry out the reallocation of produced inputs or the allocation of capital and consumption goods that will permit business enterprises to survive and grow and workers to live and attain a socially acceptable standard of living. A final implication of the breakdown of the dual price quantity relationship is that the market pricing equation based on pricing coefficients is fundamentally different from one based on production coefficients, which suggests that empirical investigations of industrial pricing based on production coefficients are flawed, that the price model does not represent the actual technological and institutional constraints of the economy, and that no substantive meaning can be attached to the term 'profit maximisation'.

Turning to the pricing model itself, a second property - the virtual absence of labour-based mark-up market pricing equations - implies that it is not possible to reduce the model to a simple mark-up on labour costs. Consequently, the Kaleckian/Weintraubian labour-based vertically integrated price models have no correspondence with economic reality, which raises the question of their relevance for macroeconomic theorising. Similarly, the model helps settle the issue as to whether it is theoretically appropriate to reduce normal cost or target rate of return pricing procedures to mark-up pricing procedures in that it can be used to show that a pure mark-up pricing model does not produce the same set of prices as a pure normal cost or target rate of return pricing model or as a general pricing model with all three pricing procedures. Therefore, not only is a pure mark-up pricing model an invalid theoretical description of economic reality; it also gives wrong 'answers'.

A third property of the model is that custom and competition are predominant among the determinants of the mark-up for profit (see Appendix 2.2, nos. 4, 7, 8, 10, 12, 20, 21, 22, 24, 25, 30, 31, 33, 34, 35, 36, 40, 42, 44, 48, 50, 51, 58, 61, 62 and Cassady (1954) for the influence of custom, convention and reasonableness and Appendix 2.2, nos. 1, 2, 4, 6, 7, 8, 11, 16, 20, 22, 24, 25, 28, 29, 30, 31, 33, 34, 35, 38, 39, 40, 41, 43, 44, 47, 50, 51, 52, 55, 56, 61, 63 for the influence of short-term and long-term competition). On the other hand, the determinants of the mark-up for profit, such as the need to finance investment, maintain and increase market share, barriers to entry and potential competition, as popularised by Post Keynesians (see the arguments of Andrews (1949), Steindl (1952) and Sylos-Labini (1969)) received little support among the pricing studies (see Appendix 2.2, nos. 1, 19, 20, 31, 34, 41, 44, 48, 55, 56, 62, 64; also see Cassady, 1954). Furthermore, as noted above, since business enterprises do not utilise an inverse price-sales relationship when making pricing decisions, the price elasticity of demand cannot be a determinant of the mark-up as well. Thus it appears that there is no empirically sustainable Post Keynesian theory of the determination of the mark-up for profit. Consequently, whatever competitive factors affect the determination of the mark-up, the role of custom and convention is significant enough to place the motivation of the price administrators outside the simple description of maximising profits (see Appendix 2.1, nos. 18, 19, 23 and Appendix 2.2, nos. 8, 22, 31, 33, 34, 40, 42, 44, 48, 55, 60; also see Shipley, 1981). Moreover, since the motivation for profits is historically specific and since capitalist societies experience varying customs and conventions and cultural lags, it is empirically and theoretically inappropriate for Post Keynesians to assume that all price administrators have the same motivation regarding the determination of the mark-up. Thus, the determinants of the mark-up for profit in the pricing model (hence the mark-up itself) must necessarily vary from market to market at a single point in time and in a particular market over time (see Appendix 2.2, nos. 4, 6, 8, 9, 14, 16, 19, 22, 23, 29, 30, 31, 34, 36, 38, 40, 41, 44, 46, 47, 48, 56, 59, 60, 61, 62, 63, 64). Finally, the persistent influence of custom and convention in the determination of the mark-up for profit undermines the Sraffian cum classical and Marxian view that a uniform rate of profit is a persistent and structural feature of a competitive capitalist economy.

A final property of the model is that its prices are tied to time, hence historical. A consequence of this is the irrelevance of the distinction found in Sraffian economics between the market price and the long-period price. Those Post Keynesians who take a Sraffian approach to price theory generally assume that the solution prices of their price model represent either long-period or quasi long-period centres of gravity to which market prices move independently of the will of the business enterprises involved, the distinction being that the former is associated with a uniform rate of profit and the latter is not. However, because the model's market prices are historical, they can move only as fast as the administered prices in the previous section did: from once every three months to less than once a year. With such a long time between each price change, it would take years for market prices to converge to quasi long-period prices. More importantly, the period of historical time needed for convergence to take place would be significantly long for wage rates, mark-ups for profit and pricing coefficients to have changed. Finally, the actual existence of perverse prices makes a mockery of the notion of convergence. With the convergence process an empirical impossibility, an unbridgeable gulf exists between the empirically grounded pricing model with its market prices and the Sraffian pricing model with its quasi long-period prices.

CONCLUSION

It was not the purpose of this chapter to demonstrate that manufacturing, wholesale and retail business enterprises used cost plus pricing procedures - the facts speak for themselves since over 80 per cent of the 4200 enterprises covered in Appendix 2.2 used such procedures. Rather, the purpose of this chapter was twofold: to develop an empirically grounded pricing model, starting with the costing and pricing procedures of the individual business enterprise and ending with a general pricing model which covers all industrial, wholesale and retail enterprises and their respective markets, and to show that the model could not be reconciled with the Kaleckian, Weintraubian and Sraffian-inspired Post Keynesian pricing models. In achieving the former, it was found that pricing procedures were quite varied and led to a variety of pricing equations, of which normal cost and target rate of return pricing equations were the most common; that most enterprises followed existing tax codes and based depreciation of plant and equipment on historical costs; that normal capacity utilisation and prices themselves were administratively determined, which meant prices changed infrequently; and that administered prices were strategic prices designed to achieve particular socially agreed goals none of which was profit maximisation.

To achieve the latter, it was argued with regard to the Kaleckian and Weintraubian models that labour and material-based pricing procedures were used by a minority of enterprises, with labour-based pricing procedures virtually not used at all; that the empirical pricing model could not be reduced to a labour-based vertically integrated industry; and that a pure mark-up pricing model produced different prices than did the empirical pricing model. As for the Sraffian pricing models, it was found that the Sraffian definition of normal capacity utilisation was either inconsistent or only partially congruent with the facts; that the Sraffian treatment of depreciation and fixed capital was also inconsistent with the facts not to mention being in violation of the tax laws hence the empirical pricing model; that the dual relationship between quantities and prices found in the Sraffian models could not occur in the empirical pricing model; that market prices in the empirical pricing model did not and could not converge to Sraffian quasi long-period prices; and that the persistent influence of custom and convention in the determination of the mark-up for profit undermined the Sraffian cum classical and Marxian view that a uniform rate of profit is a persistent and structural feature of a competitive capitalist economy.

It can also be argued that the empirical pricing model is incompatible with the theory of prices (or value) in classical political economy because many of the analytical concepts of the latter, such as supply and demand curves, equilibrium, stability, market clearing and profit maximisation (see, for example, Bharadwaj and Schefold, 1990, pp. 132, 134, 225-6, 308, 349, and 402; Dumenil and Levy, 1991; Arena, 1990; and Boggio, 1992 are not associated with the former, not to mention that market prices in the empirical pricing model would never converge to long-period prices. In addition, the majority of business enterprises do not aim to maximise the rate of profit on capital; rather they are interested in total profits, rate of profit on costs, rate of profit on sales, market share and other goals. More to the point, many enterprises do not actually have the capability to calculate the rate of profit on capital for a particular product or a whole product line, even if they did desire to maximise it, which they do not (see Appendix 2.1, nos. 20, 23; and Appendix 2.2, nos. 6, 21, 24, 33, 60, 62, 63, 64).

Finally, it must be noted that the failure of the Kaleckian, Weintraubian and Sraffian-inspired pricing models *vis-à-vis* the empirical pricing model can be largely attributed to their ahistorical nature. That is, pricing and price studies cited and referred to in this chapter clearly indicate that the former models, especially the Sraffian-inspired models, have been at odds with economic reality for the last seventy to two hundred years. Consequently, they are of little use to economists who want to examine issues of pricing and prices during the inter-war years, the post-war inflation/stagflation years, or even the entire span of the nineteenth century. If the models have no historical justification, then it stands to reason that their contemporary relevance must be very much in doubt. Although the empirically-grounded pricing model is not compatible with many of the Post Keynesian pricing models, it nevertheless does not reject the surplus approach to economics which provides the theoretical foundation of Post Keynesian economics. All that is being argued is that the surplus approach needs a new pricing model to escape the nihilistic tendencies that pervade Post Keynesian economics, for example, the use of fictionalised concepts to create a fictionalised reality. Because the model involves the rejection of much of what passes as Post Keynesian pricing theory, while implicitly and explicitly drawing on the works of G.C. Means, P.W.S. Andrews and institutionalist economists (none of whom are regarded as important contributors to Post Keynesian price theory), it cannot simply be denoted as Post Keynesian; nor can the price theory for which it is a foundation. Thus a new name is needed which reflects the wider contributions to the development of a surplus approach empirically-grounded price theory.

APPENDIX 2.1 SUMMARIES OF STUDIES ON COST ACCOUNTING AND COSTING PRACTICES

1. 'Re Cost Accounts',*The Accountant* (16 March 1907), 351.
2. 'Depreciation Policy in Manufacturing Industries', *NACA Bulletin* 17 (1 May 1936), 1053-1061.
3. Marple, R.P., 'Practice in Applying Overhead and Calculating Normal Capacity', *NACA Bulletin*, 19 (1 April 1938), 917-934.
4. US Congress. Senate. Temporary National Economic Committee. *Industrial Wage Rates, Labor Costs and Price Policies*, by Douglass V. Brown, *et al.* Senate Committee Monograph No. 5. Washington, D.C.: Government Printing Office, 1940. Also see Wonson, Harold S., 'The Use of Predetermined Costs in Pricing in the Shoe Industry', *NACA Bulletin* (1 September 1941), 28-40.
5. Black, M.L. and H.B. Eversole, *A Report on Cost Accounting in Industry*. Washington, D.C.: Government Printing Office, 1946.
6. Keller, I. Wayne (1948-49), 'Standard Manufacturing Costs for Pricing and Budgeting', *NACA Bulletin*, 30, 162-176.
7. Walkden, B. (1957), 'A consideration of some of the problems arising in the investigation of Manufacturers' costs by the Ministry of Supply from 1939 to 1945 with particular reference to methods of uniform costing to price determination in the grey cloths section of the Lancashire cotton industry and in the textile narrow fabric industry', College of Technology, York: Barnsley.
8. Langholm, O. (1965), 'Cost Structure and Costing Method: An Empirical Study', *Journal of Accounting Research*, 3, 218-227.
9. Sizer, J. (1966), 'The Accountant's Contribution to the Pricing Decision', *The Journal of Management Studies*, 3, May, 129-149.
10. Govindarajan, V. and R.N. Anthony (1983), 'How Firms Use Cost Data in Price Decisions'. *Management Accounting* (USA), July, 30-36.
11. National Association of Cost Accounts, Committee on Research (1953), 'Direct Costing', *NACA Bulletin*, 34/8, April, 1079-1128.
12. National Association of Cost Accountants, Committee on Research (1953), 'Product Costs for Pricing', *NACA Bulletin*, 34, August, 1671-1730.
13. Fog, B. (1960), *Industrial Pricing Policies*. Amsterdam: North-Holland Publishing Company.
14. Anglo-American Council on Productivity (1950), *Productivity Report*: Management Accounting. London: Anglo-American Council on Productivity.
15. Puxty, A.G. and D. Lyall (1989), *Cost Control into the 1990s: A Survey of Standard Costing and Budgeting Practices in the UK*. London: CIMA.
16. Finnie, J. and J. Sizer (1983), (ed.) by D. Cooper, R. Scapens and J. Arnold. 'The Apparent Value Placed Upon Product Cost Information in a Sample of Engineering Companies', in *Management Accounting Research and Practice*, 307-317. London: The Institute of Cost and Management Accountants.
17. Scapens, R.W., M.Y. Gameil and D.J. Cooper (1983), (ed.) by D. Cooper, R. Scapens and J. Arnold, 'Accounting Information for Pricing Decisions: An

Empirical Study', in *Management Accounting Research and Practice*, 283-306. London: The Institute of Cost and Management Accountants.

18.   Coates, J.B., J.E. Smith and R.J. Stacey (1983), (ed.) by D. Cooper, R. Scapens and J. Arnold, 'Results of a Preliminary Survey into the Structure of Divisionalised Companies, Divisionalised Performance Appraisal and the Associated Role of Management Accounting', in *Management Accounting Research and Practice*, 265-282. London: The Institute of Cost and Management Accountants.

19.   Innes, J. and F. Mitchell (1989), *Management Accounting: The Challenge of Technological Innovation*. London: CIMA.

20.   Howe, M. (1961), 'Accounting Information and Product Decisions in the Multi-Product Firm'. Ph.D. dissertation, University of Sheffield.

21.   Laudeman, M. and F.W. Schaeberle (1983), 'The Cost Accounting Practices of Firms Using Standard Costs', *Cost and Management* (Canada), July-August, 21-25.

22.   National Association of Accountants (1958), *Current Practice in Accounting for Depreciation*. Research Report (No. 33). New York City: National Association of Accountants.

23.   Hart, H. and D.F. Prusmann (1963), *A Report of a Survey of Management Accounting Techniques in the S.E. Hants Coastal Region*. Southampton: University of Southampton.

APPENDIX 2.2 SUMMARIES OF STUDIES IN PRICING

1.   Brown, D. (1924), 'Pricing Policy in Relation to Financial Control', *Management and Administration*, 7, 195-198, 283-286, and 417-422. Also see Vanderblue, H.B. (1939), 'Pricing Policies in the Automobile Industry', *Harvard Business Review*, 17, 385-401; Vanderblue, H.B. (1939-1940) 'Pricing Policies in the Automobile Industry: Incidence of Demand', *Harvard Business Review*, 18, 64-81; Kaplan, A.D.H., J.B. Dirlam and R.F. Lanzillotti (1958), *Pricing in Big Business: A Case Approach*. Washington D.C.: The Brookings Institution; Hutton, W.T. (1959), 'Price Formulation and Price Behavior in Three Heavy Manufacturing Industries'. Ph.D. dissertation, Ohio State University; and Johnson, H.T. (1978), 'Management Accounting in an Early Multidivisional Organisation: General Motors in the 1920s'. *Business History Review*, 52, 490-517.

2.   Churchill, W.L. (1932), *Pricing for Profit*. New York: The Macmillan Company.

3.   Agnew, H.E. (1935), 'Fundamentals of Price Making', New York University.

4.   Hall, R.L. and C.J. Hitch (1939), 'Price Theory and Business Behaviour', *Oxford Economic Papers*, 2, 12-45.

5.   US Congress (1940), Senate. Temporary National Economic Committee. *Industrial Wage Rates, Labor Costs and Price Policies*, by D.V. Brown, *et al*. Senate Committee Print, Monograph No. 5, Washington, D.C.: Government Printing Office; US Federal Trade Commission (1938), *Report on the Agricultural Implement and Machinery Industry*. Washington, D.C.: Government Printing Office; and Conant, M. (1949), 'Aspects of Monopoly and Price Policies in the Farm Machinery Industry Since 1902'. Ph.D. dissertation, University of Chicago. Also see Kaplan, A.D.H., J.B. Dirlam and R.F. Lanzillotti (1958), *Pricing in Big*

Business: A Case Approach. Washington, D.C.: The Brookings Institution; and Park, J.C.S. (1959), 'Value Theory and Oligopolistic Manufacturing Industries'. Ph.D. dissertation, University of Nebraska.

6. Saxton, C.C. (1942), *The Economics of Price Determination*. Oxford: Oxford University Press.

7. Thompson, G.C. (1947), 'How Industry Prices Its Products'. *The Conference Board Business Record*, 4, 180-182.

8. The Dartnell Report (1949), *Pricing Policies*. Special Investigation Report 572. Chicago: The Dartnell Corporation.

9. Alt, R.M (1949), 'The Internal Organisation of the Firm and Price Formation: An Illustrative Case', *Quarterly Journal of Economics*, 63, 92-110.

10. Hague, D.C. (1949-1950), 'Economic Theory and Business Behaviour', *The Review of Economic Studies*, 16, 144-157.

11. Saville, Lloyd Blackstone (1950), 'Price Determination in the Gray-Iron-Foundry Industry'. Ph.D. dissertation, Columbia University.

12. Dean, J. and Th. Yntema (1951), National Bureau of Economic Research Committee of the Conference on Price Research, 1941-1951. Cited in Dean, J., *Managerial Economics*. Englewood Cliffs, New Jersey: Prentice-Hall Inc.

13. Woodruff, W. (1953), 'Early Entrepreneurial Behaviour in Relation to Costs and Prices', *Oxford Economic Papers*, 5, 41-64.

14. Blackwell, R. (1953-1954), 'The Pricing of Books', *Journal of Industrial Economics*, 2, 174-183.

15. Cook, A. and E. Jones (1954), 'Full Cost Pricing in Western Australia', *The Economic Record*, 30, 272-274.

16. Kohl, M. (1954), 'The Role of Accounting in Pricing'. Ph.D. dissertation, Columbia University.

17. Shackle, G.L.S. (1955), 'Business Men on Business Decisions', *Scottish Journal of Political Economy*, 2, 32-46; and Brown, C.V. (1967), 'Special Seminar Report', Glasgow University, Management Studies, 1-13.

18. Hinton, B. J. (1955), 'An Economic Analysis of Selected Factors in Industrial Pricing Techniques'. Ph.D. dissertation, Louisiana State University.

19. Great Britain (1955), The Monopolies and Restrictive Practices Commission. *Report on the Supply and Export of Certain Semi-Manufacturers of Copper and Copper-Based Alloys*.

20. Cook, A.C., N.F. Dufty and E.H. Jones (1956), 'Full Cost Pricing in the Multi-Product Firm', *The Economic Record*, 32, 142-147.

21. Great Britain (1956), The Monopolies and Restrictive Practices Commission. *Report on the Supply of Hard Fibre Cordage*.

22. Great Britain (1956), The Monopolies and Restrictive Practices Commission. *Report on the Supply of Standard Metal Windows and Doors*.

23. Pearce, I.F. (1956), 'A Study in Price Policy', *Economica*, 23, 114-127.

24. Pearce, I.F. and L.R. Amey (1956-1957), 'Price Policy with a Branded Product', *The Review of Economic Studies*, 4, 49-60.

25. Lazer, W. (1956-1957), 'Price Determination in the Western Canadian Garment Industry', *The Journal of Industrial Economics*, 5, 124-136.

26. Balkin, N. (1956-1957), 'Prices in the Clothing Industry', *The Journal of Industrial Economics*, 5, 1-15.

27. Karger, Th. and G.C. Thompson (1957), 'Pricing Policies and Practices', *The Conference Board Business Record*, 14, 434-442.

28. Ross, R.B. *et al.* (1958), *Pricing for Profit in Competitive Markets*. Dartnell Management Report 606. Chicago: The Dartnell Corporation.

29. Lydall, H.F. (1958), 'Aspects of Competition in Manufacturing Industry', *Institute of Economics and Statistics Bulletin*, 20, 319-337.

30. Pool, A.G. and G. Llewellyn (1958), *The British Hosiery Industry: A Study in Competition*. Leicester: Leicester University Press.

31. Brookings Institution Investigation of Pricing Practices: Kaplan, A.D.H. (1958), *Big Enterprise in a Competitive System*. Washington, D.C.: The Brookings Institution. Kaplan, A.D H., J.B. Dirlam and R.F. Lanzillotti (1958), *Pricing in Big Business: A Case Approach*. Washington, D.C.: The Brookings Institution. Lanzillotti, R.F. (1958), 'Pricing Objectives in Large Companies', *The American Economic Review*, 48, 921-940.

32. Parks, J.C.S. (1959), 'Value Theory and Oligopolistic Manufacturing Industries'. Ph.D. dissertation, University of Nebraska.

33. Great Britain (1959), The Monopolies Commission. *Report on the Supply of Chemical Fertilisers*.

34. Fog, B. (1960), *Industrial Pricing Policies: An Analysis of Pricing Policies of Danish Manufacturing*. Amsterdam: North-Holland Publishing Company. Also see (1948), 'Price Theory and Reality', *Nordisk Tidsskrift for Teknisk Okonomi*, 12, 89-94.

35. Kempner, T. (1960), 'Costs and Prices in Launderetts', *Journal of Industrial Economics*, 8, 216-229.

36. Haynes, W. W. (1962), *Pricing Decisions in Small Business*. Lexington: University of Kentucky Press. Haynes, W. W. (1964), 'Pricing Practices in Small Firms', *The Southern Economic Journal*, 30, 315-324.

37. Eliot, G. (1963), 'Analysis of Small Manufacturers, Pricing Policies in Southern California'. Ph.D. dissertation, University of Southern California.

38. Fitzpatrick, A.A. (1964), *Pricing Methods of Industry*. Boulder, Colorado: Pruett Press, Inc.

39. Lanzillotti, R. (1964), *Pricing, Production, and Marketing Policies of Small Manufacturers*. Pullman, Washington: Washington State University.

40. Barback, R.H. (1964), *The Pricing of Manufacturers*. London: Macmillan and Co. Ltd.

41. Knox, R.L. (1966), 'Competitive Oligopolistic Pricing', *Journal of Marketing*, 30, 47-51. Also see Hutton, W.T. (1959), 'Price Formation and Price Behavior in Three Heavy Manufacturing Industries', Ohio State University; and Kaplan, A.D H., J.B. Dirlam and R.F. Lanzillotti (1958), *Pricing in Big Business: A Case Approach*. Washington, D.C.: The Brookings Institution.

42. Long, W.F.E. (1967-1968), 'Formula Pricing to Reduce Technological Uncertainty: A Case Study in Computer Transistors', *Antitrust Law & Economics Review*, 1, 131-156.

43. Skinner, R.C. (1969-1970), 'The Determination of Selling Prices', *Journal of Industrial Economics*, 18, 201-217. Also see Sizer, J. (1971-1972) 'Note on "The Determination of Selling Prices"', *Journal of Industrial Economics*, 20, 85-89.

44. Howe, M. (1960), 'Competition and the Multiplication of Products', *Yorkshire Bulletin of Economic and Social Research*, 12, 57-72; 'Accounting Information and Product Decisions in the Multi-Product Firm'. Ph.D. dissertation, University of Sheffield, 1961; 'The Restrictive Practices Court and the Definition of the Market', *The Manchester School of Economic and Social Studies*, 34 (1966), 41-61; 'The Iron and Steel Board and Steel Pricing, 1953-1967', *Scottish Journal of Political Economy*, 15 (1968), 43-67; and 'A Study of Trade Association Price Fixing', *Journal of Industrial Economics*, 21 (1972-1973), 236-256.

45. Rosendale, P.B. (1973), 'The Short-Run Pricing Policies of Some British Engineering Exporters'. *National Institute Economic Review*, 65, 44-51.

46. Atkin, B. and R. Skinner (1976), *How British Industry Prices*. London: Industrial Market Research Limited.

47. Holmes, P.M. (1978), *Industrial Pricing Behaviour and Devaluation*. London: The Macmillan Press Ltd.

48. Hankinson, A. (1985), *Pricing Behaviour: A Study of Pricing Behaviour of Dorset-Hampshire Small Engineering Firms 1983-1985*. Dorset Institute of Higher Education; also see *Output Determination: A Study of Output Determination of Dorset-Hampshire Small Engineering Firms 1983-1985*. Dorset Institute of Higher Education.

49. Jerron, A.M (1960). 'Conversion Costs'. *The Cost Accountant*, 38, 56.

50. Gordon, L.A., R. Cooper, H. Falk and D. Miller (1981), *The Pricing Decision*. New York City: National Association of Accountants.

51. Raine, G.F. (1965), (ed.), *The Woollen and Worsted Industry: An Economic Analysis*. Oxford: Clarendon Press.

52. Wentz, Th. (1966), 'Realism in Pricing Analyses', *Journal of Marketing*, 30, 19-26.

53. Likierman, A. (1981), 'Pricing Policy in the Texturising Industry, 1958-71', *The Journal of Industrial Economics*, 30, 25-38.

54. Goetz, J.F. (1985), 'The Pricing Decision: A Service Industry's Experience', *Journal of Small Business Management*, 23, 61-67.

55. Hague, D.C. (1971), *Pricing in Business*. London: George Allen & Unwin Ltd.

56. Wied-Nebbeling, S. (1975), *Industrielle Preissetzung*. Tubingen. Wied-Nebbeling, (1985), *Das Preisverhalten in der Industrie*. Tubingen. Wied-Nebbeling, S. (1992), Personal communication. 1 January.

57. Mills, R.W. and Chr. Sweeting (1988), *Pricing Decisions in Practice*. London: CIMA.

58. Price Commission (1979), *Prices, Costs and Margins in the Distribution of Video Tape Recorders and their Accessories*. London: HMSO.

59. Price Commission (1978b), *Prices, Costs and Margins in the Distribution of Footwear in the United Kingdom*. London: HMSO.

60. Price Commission (1978c), *Prices, Costs and Margins in the Publishing, Printing and Binding, and Distribution of Books*. London: HMSO.

61. Price Commission (1978), *The Pricing of Beds*. London: HMSO.

62. Abe, K. and M. Kometani (1985), 'Behavioural Style of Modern Japanese Big Business'. The Economic Society of Yamaguchi University, in Japanese. Summarised and translated by T. Kanao.
63. Sakurai, M. and K. Ito (1986), 'An Empirical Research about Price Determination of Japanese Firms'. *Accounting*, in Japanese. Summarised and translated by T. Kanao.
64. Hague, D.C., W.E.F. Oakeshott and A.A. Strain (1977), *Devaluation and Pricing Decisions: A Case Study Approach*. London: George Allen and Unwin, Ltd.

APPENDIX 2.3 SUMMARIES OF STUDIES ON THE FREQUENCY OF PRICE CHANGES

1. Carlton, D.W. (1968), 'The Rigidity of Prices', *The American Economic Review*, 76, 637-658.
2. Kashyap, A.K. (1988), 'Setting and Investment: Models and Evidence'. Ph.D. dissertation, Massachusetts Institute of Technology.
3. Blinder, A.S. (1991), 'Why are Prices Sticky? Preliminary Results from an Interview Study', *American Economic Review*, 81, 89-96.
4. Wilson, Ch. (1954), *The History of Unilever: A Study in Economic Growth and Social Change*, Vols. I & II. London: Cassell & Company Ltd.

NOTES

The author is grateful to P. Earl, I. Steedman, P. Skott and L. Boggio for comments on an earlier draft of this chapter.

1. Shop expenses are defined as those expenses related to the production of a particular product line and generally include the salaries of foremen, support staff and supervisors; the materials needed to maintain the support staff and the technical efficiency of the plant and equipment used directly in production; and the depreciation allowance associated with the plant and equipment.

2. Firm expenses are defined as those expenses which are common to all product lines but specific to none and are necessary if the business enterprise is to stay in existence as a going concern. In general, these costs are associated with those activities which the firm must engage in order to coordinate the production flows of the various product lines, to sell the various products, and to develop and implement enterprise-wide investment and diversification plans. These include the salaries of management, office expenses, insurance, selling costs and the depreciation of the central office buildings and equipment.

3. Empirical evidence for the existence of perverse prices can be found in Means (1972) and Blair (1972, 1974). Evidence from the 1930s is relatively scarce, but examples of perverse prices do exist for some products including boiler tubes, cigarettes, sodium sulphide, concrete bricks, electric ranges and sewing machines.

Dynamics of the firm

4.   This necessarily means that administered prices are not market-clearing prices; nor do they vary with each change in sales (or shift in the virtually non-existent market or enterprises ('demand curve'). For further discussion, see Lee 1984, 1985 and 1990-91.
5.   According to the studies in Appendix 2.2 (also see Choksi, 1979), the enterprises did not base their decisions to alter their prices on the status of their sales. That is, the enterprises did not increase their prices if sales were above normal and nor did they reduce their prices if sales were below normal. Thus, there exists no empirical support for the pricing behaviour postulated in the cross dual-price models of classical political economy.

REFERENCES

Andrews, P.W.S. (1949), *Manufacturing Business*. London: Macmillan & Co. Ltd.

Arena, R. (1990), 'Are Classical Economic Dynamics Still Useful in the Nineties?' Unpublished.

Bell, C.S. (1960), 'On the Elasticity of Demand at Retail', *The American Journal of Economics and Sociology,* 20, 63-72.

Bharadwaj, K. and B. Schefold (eds.) (1990), *Essays on Piero Sraffa: Critical Perspectives on the Revival of Classical Theory*. London: Unwin Hyman.

Blair, J.M. (1972), *Economic Concentration: Structure, Behavior and Public Policy*. New York: Harcourt Brace Jovanovich, Inc.

Blair, J.M. (1974), 'Market Power and Inflation: A Short-Run Target Return Model', *Journal of Economic Issues,* 8, June, 453-477.

Boggio, L. (1992), 'Production Prices and Dynamic Stability: Results and Open Questions', *The Manchester School of Economic and Social Studies,* 60, September, 264-294.

Cassady, R. (1954), *Price Making and Price Behavior in the Petroleum Industry*. New Haven: Yale University Press.

Chandler, A.D. (1962), *Strategy and Structure*. Cambridge: MIT Press.

Chandler, A.D. (1977), *The Visible Hand*. Cambridge: Harvard University Press.

Choksi, S. (1979), 'Pricing Policies in the Canadian Copper, Aluminium, Nickel, and Steel Industries'. Ph.D. dissertation, McGill University.

Ciccone, R. (1987), 'Accumulation, Capacity Utilisation and Distribution: a Reply', *Political Economy: Studies in the Surplus Approach,* 3, 97-111.

Ciccone, R. (1990), (ed.) by K. Bharadwaj and B. Schefold. 'Accumulation and Capacity Utilisation: Some Critical Considerations on Joan Robinson's Theory of Distribution', in *Essays on Piero Sraffa*, 417-429. London: Unwin Hyman.

Clifton, J.A. (1983), 'Administered Prices in the Context of Capitalist Development', *Contributions to Political Economy,* 2, March, 23-38.

Dumenil, G. and D. Levy (1991), 'Convergence to Long-Period Positions, with the Benefit of Hindsight', CEPREMAP, LAREA-CEDRA, Paris.

Dutt, A.K. (1988), 'Competition, Monopoly Power and the Prices of Production', *Thames Papers in Political Economy,* Autumn, 1-29.

Eichner, A.S. (1991), *The Macrodynamics of Advanced Market Economies*. Armonk, New York: M.E. Sharpe, Inc.

Gordon, R.A. (1945), *Business Leadership in the Large Corporation*. Washington, D.C.: The Brookings Institution.

Harcourt, G.C. and P. Kenyon (1976), 'Pricing and the Investment Decision', *Kyklos*, 29, 449-477.

Hodgkins, P. (1979), (ed.) by T.A. Lee and R.H. Parker. 'Unilever - The First 21 Years' in *The Evolution of Corporate Financial Reporting*, 40-46. Sunbury-on-Thames: Thomas Nelson and Sons Ltd.

Kalecki, M. (1954), *Theory of Economic Dynamics*. London: George Allen & Unwin.

Kregel, J.A. (1975), *The Reconstruction of Political Economy: An Introduction to Post-Keynesian Economics*, 2nd ed. London: The Macmillan Press Ltd.

Kurz, H.D. (1986), 'Normal Positions and Capital Utilisation', *Political Economy: Studies in the Surplus Approach*, 2, 37-54.

Kurz, H.D. (1990), (ed.) by K. Bharadwaj and B. Schefold. 'Accumulation, Distribution and the 'Keynesian Hypothesis', in *Essays on Piero Sraffa: Critical Perspectives on the Revival of Classical Theory*, 396-413. London: Unwin Hyman.

Lee, F.S. (1984), 'Full Cost Pricing: A New Wine in a New Bottle', *Australian Economic Papers*, 24, June, 151-166.

Lee, F.S. (1985), 'Full Cost Prices, Classical Price Theory, and Long Period Analysis: A Critical Evaluation', *Metroeconomica*, 37, 199-219.

Lee, F.S. (1986), 'Post Keynesian View of Average Direct Costs: A Critical Evaluation of the Theory and the Empirical Evidence', *Journal of Post Keynesian Economics*, 8, Spring, 400-424.

Lee, F.S. (1990-91), 'Marginalist Controversy and Post Keynesian Price Theory', *Journal of Post Keynesian Economics*, 13, Winter, 252-263.

Means, G.C. (1939), *The Structure of the American Economy*. Part I: *Basic Characteristics*. Washington, D.C.: GPO.

Means, G.C. (1972), 'The Administered-Price Thesis Reconfirmed', *The American Economic Review*, 62, June, 292-306.

Means, G.C. (1983), 'Corporate Power in the Market Place', *The Journal of Law and Economics*, 24, June, 467-485.

Nobes, C. (1985), *Depreciation Problems in the Context of Historic Cost Accounting*. London: Certified Accountant Publications Limited.

Nourse, E.G. (1944), *Price Making in a Democracy*. Washington, D.C.: The Brookings Institution.

Nourse, E.G. and H.B. Drury (1938), *Industrial Price Policies and Economic Progress*, Washington, D.C.: The Brookings Institution.

Ong, N.-P. (1981), 'Target Pricing, Competition, and Growth', *Journal of Post Keynesian Economics*, 4, Fall 101-116.

Sawyer, M.C. (1990), 'Prices, Pricing and Growth: An Attempted Synthesis', Unpublished.

Select Committee on National Expenditure (1941), *Fourth Report*, The House of Commons, Session 1940-41, London: HMSO.

Semmler, W. (1984), *Competition, Monopoly, and Differential Profit Rates*, New York: Columbia University Press.

Shipley, D.D. (1981), 'Pricing Objectives in British Manufacturing Industry'. *The Journal of Industrial Economics*, 29, 429-443.

Simon, H.A. *et al.* (1954), *Centralisation vs. Decentralisation in Organising the Controller's Department*, New York: Controllership Foundation.

Steindl, J. (1952), *Maturity and Stagnation in American Capitalism*. Oxford: Basil Blackwell.

Sylos-Labini, P. (1969), *Oligopoly and Technical Progress*, Revised Edition. Cambridge: Harvard University Press.

Vangermeersch, R. (1979), (ed.) by T.A. Lee and R.H. Parker. 'A Historical Overview of Depreciation: US Steel 1902-1970', in *The Evolution of Corporate Financial Reporting*, 64-79. Sunbury-on-Thames: Thomas Nelson and Sons Ltd.

3. Corporate Networks: A US Case Study

F. Gregory Hayden and Kurt Stephenson

INTRODUCTION

Network studies explain that cooperation among firms seems to occur more and more. 'The cooperation phenomenon forces researchers to focus on the widespread and complex interdependencies between firms in the economy' (Beije and Groenewegen, 1992, p. 88). The extended interdependencies lead to a structural network. 'The strength of a network is that activities at various places can be performed on the basis of complementary resources from many actors. In this way, chains of interconnected activities are established. Activity chains consist of both transaction and transformation activities' (Beije and Groenewegen, 1992, p. 96). Therefore, 'network analysis of markets tries to describe the complex processes that establish the structure ... and the undercurrent of its development' (Beije and Groenewegen, 1992, p. 88).

This chapter will address a number of issues; however, its overarching purpose is to explain how the Social Fabric Matrix (SFM) can be utilised to describe and analyse the complex and overlapping relationships among corporations (Appendix 3.1 contains a glossary of acronyms and symbols). Numerous studies in sociology, management science and economics have been conducted, providing a variety of analyses regarding the overlapping nature of corporate directorships. Directorship data are used as the vehicle to demonstrate the SFM. More important than the case study presented on translocking[1] corporate directorships is the emphasis that the SFM can be used for other deliveries, exchanges and overlaps among corporations. A number of articles have been published on the description of the components and the SFM (Hayden,

1982; Groenewegen and Beije, 1989; Meister, 1990). A brief explanation will be sufficient for our purposes here.

The SFM is a technical methodology which is based on theoretical and technical developments in numerous areas. It was developed to allow for the convergence and integration of conceptual frameworks in systems analysis, institutional economics, boolean algebra, social system analysis, ecology and geobased data systems. The focus of the SFM is to provide a tool which will integrate diverse scientific literature and diverse kinds of data bases. In this way it is possible to describe a system, articulate knowledge gaps in the system for future research, evaluate policies, opportunities and crises within the system, and create a data base for future monitoring. The SFM was developed because the scientific literature indicated that a narrow conceptualisation of economic systems was not viable.

Before it is possible to assemble a framework for defining the relationships contained in a problem area, it is necessary to identify the components. Studies in anthropology, social psychology, economics and ecology suggest that seven major components need to be identified and integrated. They are as follows: (1) cultural values, (2) societal beliefs, (3) personal attitudes, (4) personal tastes, (5) natural environment, (6) technology and (7) social institutions (Hayden, 1982). The case study presented below collects data regarding only one of the seven components, an institutional one. The institution of concern is the overlap of directors among various corporations, often referred to as a mediating institution by sociologists. The goal is to explain how to use the SFM to identify and derive networks and centralised patterns of overlap.

OVERLAP AND REACHABILITY CONCEPTS

Conceptually, the concern is with the overlapping sets that define the network and delivery process.[2] This can be explained with the use of the simple digraph (directed graph) in Figure 3.1. Assume that E, F, G, H and I are five organisations, five different corporations in our case. Corporations can make various kinds of deliveries to each other. In this case we will be concerned with the delivery of directors. The deliveries among the organisations, for example directors D_1 through D_7 in Figure 3.1, are an important part of their transorganisational relationships. The importance, or central position, of any corporation would depend on the number of different kinds of transorganisational sets in which it is involved, and on the number of deliveries within each set. If two corporations each send one director to the other's board, the degree of overlap would be less than if the same corporations shared four directors.

Figure 3.1 Organisation overlap and reachability digraph

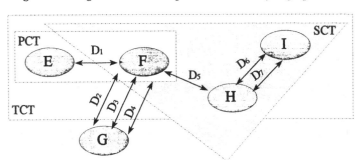

Let us begin by specifying three different kinds of organisational overlap sets. They are primary, secondary and tertiary sets, bounded in Figure 3.1 to outline each set.

Primary Overlap: A primary corporate translock (PCT) is outlined in Figure 3.1 by the rectangle around E and F. As indicated, director D_1 serves on the boards of corporations E and F. Corporation E is involved in one PCT with F and has one primary director translock (PDT). The PDT indicates the delivery level (number delivered). Although not outlined by a dotted line in Figure 3.1, other PCT sets include those between G and F, F and H, and H and I. Corporation G, for example, has one PCT and three PDTs with corporation F. With a primary overlap, the directors on the two governing boards meet together at each other's board meetings to plan jointly for the two corporations involved.

Secondary Overlap: A secondary corporate translock (SCT) is outlined in Figure 3.1 by a set (enclosed by a triangle) which includes corporations F, H and I. Corporation I has a SCT with corporation F through corporation H. This example of a SCT has three secondary director translocks (SDTs), which are D_5, D_6 and D_7. Other SCT sets in Figure 3.1 include E with G and G with H. With a secondary overlap, the directors on the two governing boards are still meeting face-to-face in planning sessions on a third governing board, which has an overlapping interest in the two SCT corporations. There are direct planning relationships between the two companies, and the directors involved have direct face-to-face reachability with regard to decisions in a deliberative setting.

Tertiary Overlap: A tertiary corporate translock (TCT) is outlined in Figure 3.1 by a rectangle set that includes corporations E, F, H and I. Corporation E has a TCT with corporation I through corporations F and H. This example of a TCT has four tertiary director translocks (TDTs). They are D_1, D_5, D_6 and D_7. Unlike primary and secondary corporate overlaps, there are not necessarily direct face-to-face relationships at a governing board meeting between the directors from E and I. To use the example in Figure 3.1, after D_1 and D_5 meet at corporation F, deliberative decisions and plans, if they are to include corporation I, must take place at the board meeting of corporation H. E has reachability to I, but it can be once removed from direct face-to-face planning deliberations, as indicated in Figure 3.1. Another TCT in Figure 3.1 is G with I though F and H, with six TDTs. The TDTs are D_2, D_3, D_4, D_5, D_6 and D_7.

Figure 3.1 is, of course, too limited to portray all the various sets of corporations in a real world context. We can observe from Figure 3.1, however, that corporation F is a central organisation in the process network. It is involved in more organisational overlap sets and has more reachability to other corporations, as well as a greater level of deliveries in terms of directors, than any other corporation. This is because it lies in the intersection of all three sets.

EXTENSION WITH THE SOCIAL FABRIC MATRIX AND DIGRAPH

The Social Fabric Matrix (SFM) can be used to extend the organisational overlap concepts and to apply them to the complex and 'redundant' overlaps of the real world. To explain this application of the SFM, corporations A, B, C, J and K are arrayed along both sides of the matrix in Table 3.1, with the delivery of directors from one corporation to another being indicated in the cells. For example, corporation A delivers its board member X to the board of corporation B, and member Z to corporation J. As another example, C delivers Y to B and Z to J, while two members, N and M, are sent to K.

The rows and columns can be aggregated as in Table 3.1, and thus the various overlaps defined above are specified in the matrix as follows:

PCT: The total PCTs a corporation has with other corporations is the total number of cells with entries in the corporation's row in the SFM. For example, the row total for cell entries for corporation C is 3.

PDT: The total PDTs involved in a corporation's PCTs is the total number of directors in a corporation's row. For example, the row total for directors for corporation C is 4.

SCT: The total SCTs a corporation has with other corporations is the total number of cells with entries, less 1, in the column, for columns with a corporation's director delivery to a PCT. For example, the total SCTs for corporation A can be found by the aggregation of the cell entries of columns 2 and 4, less 1 for each column. Or, corporation A is involved in 5 SCTs [(3—1) + (4—1) = 5]. To find the SCTs for A, read across the row from left to right (as indicated by the directed dashed line). In column 2, director X from A is serving on the board of B (a PCT). If we read down, it will be discovered that corporations C and J also deliver Y and N respectively to the board of B. Thus, A has a SCT with C and another with J through B. Because B is the direct PCT through which the SCTs with C and J are accomplished, it is not counted in the total. A similar SCT case exists in column 4.

Table 3.1 Social fabric matrix of corporate direct deliveries

Delivering Corporations \ Receiving Corporations	(1) A	(2) B	(3) C	(4) J	(5) K	(6) Total Entries	(7) Row Total
(1) A → →	→ → →	→↓ X		Z		2	2
(2) B		X ↓	Y	N		3	3
(3) C	← ← ←	←↓ Y →↦	→ → →	↦ Z →ǀ→	N,M →↦	3	4
(4) J		Z	↓ N	Z		I	4	4
(5) K			↓	N,M	I		2	3
(6) Total Entries		2	3	3	4	2		
(7) Column Totals		2	3	4	4	3		

SDT: The total SDTs participating in a corporation's SCTs is the total number of directors in the column that contains a corporation's delivery of directors to a PCT. For example, the total SDT for corporation A can be found by the aggregation of the cell entries of columns 2 and 4, for a total of 7. To find the SDT total for A, read across the row from left to right. In column 2, director X serves on the board of B. All of the directors in column 2 are members of the SDT. A similar SDT case exists in column 4, in which there are 4 SDTs.

TCT: The total TCTs to which a corporation belongs is the total number of cells with entries, less 1, for rows in which there is a corporation with which the original corporation has a SCT. For example, the total TCTs for corporation A can be found by the aggregation of the cell entries, less 1, for each row, for rows 3 and 4. Or, stated differently, corporation A participated in 5 TCTs [(3-1) + (4-1) = 5] through corporation B. To find a TCT for A, read across row 1 (still following the directed dashed line) from left to right to a PCT (column 2), go down that column to a SCT, and then aggregate all the cell entries in that row (row 3) minus 1. The 1 is subtracted in that row for the SCT through which the TCT is formed. A similar TCT case exists for row 4. This calculation would need to be repeated (not indicated by dashed lines in Table 3.1) for each SCT through corporation J in column 4 to obtain the total number of TCTs for corporation A, or 5 TCTs [(3-1) + (3-1) + (2-1) = 5]. Thus, the total TCTs for corporation A is 10 [5+5].

TDT: The total TDTs are the total number of directors in the TCT rows plus the number of directors in the PCT cell from which each TCT originates. For example, the total for corporation A is 23. To find the TCT total for A, read across the row from left to right. There is 1 director in PCT cell (1,2). Reading down from cell (1,2), row 3 has 4 directors plus the 1 director in cell (1,2). A similar process is followed for row 4. Reading down from cell (1,4), row 2 has 3 directors plus the 1 director in cell (1,4) from which the TCT in row 2 originates. A similar process is followed for rows 3 and 5. Thus [(4+1) + (4+1) + (3+1) + (4+1)+ (3+1)] = 23.

The matrix in Table 3.1 is laid out in digraph format in Figure 3.2, which clarifies reachability and redundancy. By studying Figure 3.2, it is more obvious that corporation A was able to reach J through numerous channels: with a direct PCT, with a SCT through B, and with a TCT through B and C. These redundant linkages enhance the opportunity for decisions and plans to be coordinated and implemented conjointly. These are redundant reinforcement channels. Equally important, all those corporations reach A. Stated differently, A reaches itself indirectly through these linkages. At first blush this statement may sound irrelevant. Yet, upon reflection, it means that the directors delivered to A's board from other corporations can remind A of A's original decisions and other corporations' reliance on those original decisions, reinforcing plans that lead to continuity of the economic process. This planning transmission cycle is consistent with the institutional theory of cumulative circular causation.

Figure 3.2 Social fabric digraph of corporate director deliveries

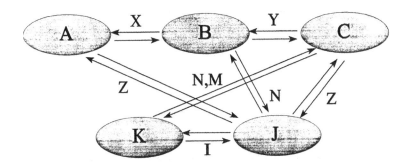

NEBRASKA CORPORATIONS

To demonstrate the matrix and digraph in a real world setting, all those corporations with their home office headquarters in the State of Nebraska in the United States were used as a SFM case study by Hayden and Stephenson (1992). To articulate the network process of organisation overlap among private corporations in Nebraska, they collected directorship data on 348 Nebraska corporations.

Pattern of Nebraska Corporate Overlap

To discover the pattern of overlapping governing boards, those corporations with at least one PCT were entered into a Social Fabric Matrix. The list included 100 corporations, thus requiring a matrix of 100 rows and 100 columns. The number of directors from each corporation that served on another board were entered into the relevant matrix cells, and the PCTs, PDTs, SCTs, SDTs, TCTs and TDTs were aggregated in the type of matrix explained above and illustrated in Table 3.1. The results of the aggregation for those corporations with four or more PCTs are rank ordered in columns 1 and 2 of Table 3.2, along with the number of PDTs in column 3. There were 30 corporations with four or more PCTs. FirsTier Financial, the top ranked in direct board connections, had 30 PCTs and 42 PDTs. This means that FirsTier had at least one of its directors serving on 30 other Nebraska corporation boards; on the boards of other corporations, FirsTier held 42 board positions.

In determining director deliveries among boards, board members of subsidiary corporations were included as members of the parent corporation's board. This was done in order not to increase the apparent number of translocks of particular boards and members. Board members from the parent company are often on the subsidiary board. This arrangement was not considered as constituting a separate corporate overlap because these members all belong to the same corporation. Had such internal deliveries of board members been counted, the totals in Table 3.2 would have multiplied considerably.

Ranking by number of SCTs is given in columns 4 and 5 of Table 3.2. The corporations with 30 or more SCTs are listed. Column 6 contains their corresponding number of SDTs. Of interest are the corporations that did not make the PCT and PDT list, but which are included in the SCT and SDT list. They are Farmers Mutual Insurance, Woodmen Accident and Life, Mutual of Omaha Insurance Co., IBP, Mall Corp. and the Nebraska Farmer (all indicated with an asterisk in Table 3.2, column 4). These are all corporations which were connected via a PCT to FirsTier. Any corporation with a PCT to FirsTier would automatically be involved with at least 29 SCTs. This reveals that a corporation can be well connected and prominent in the system without a large number of PCTs if those it has are with other central corporations. As an example, Mutual of Omaha has only three PCTs, but one is with FirsTier. The reverse of that situation can be seen with First National of Nebraska, parent of First National-Omaha. First National of Nebraska appears in column 1, but not in columns 4 or 7. It does not have a PCT with FirsTier Financial or with other central corporations; thus it does not generate enough SCTs to qualify for the list in column 4.

Ranking by number of TCTs appears in columns 7 and 8 of Table 3.2. Those corporations with 170 or more TCTs are listed. Column 9 contains their corresponding number of TDTs. As with the SCT ranking, there are corporations in the top 26 with respect to their number of TCTs that are not listed in columns 1 and 4 (as indicated by an asterisk). Of greater interest, the SFM allows us to discover the large number of other corporations that any one corporation can reach on a tertiary basis. For example, FirsTier, with 30 PCTs, is involved in 447 tertiary board overlaps and has 886 TDTs.

Nebraska Central Planning Core

Hayden and Stephenson (1992) identified 15 corporations as the most central corporations in the Nebraska economy and identified these

Table 3.2 Ranking of Nebraska corporations by director overlap sets, 1988-89

Ranking by PCT			Ranking by SCT			Ranking by TCT		
(1) Corporation	(2) PCT	(3) PDT	(4) Corporation	(5) SCT	(6) SDT	(7) Corporation	(8) TCT	(9) TDT
FirsTier Financial	30	42	FirsTier Financial	105	179	Lincoln Telecommunications	562	1058
LincolnTelecommunications	15	21	Lincoln Telecommunications	98	154	Ameritas Life Ins. Corp.	480	922
First Commerce Bancshares	14	20	Ameritas Life Ins. Corp.	90	131	FirsTier Financial	447	886
Ameritas Life Ins. Corp.	11	15	First Commerce Bancshares	78	129	First Commerce Bancshares	390	723
Norwest Bank-Nebraska	9	11	Valmont Industries	68	110	Valmont Industries	388	764
Packers Bank and Trust	9	11	Packers Bank and Trust	55	83	Bank of Norfolk	349	586
Bank of Norfolk	8	8	Farmers Mutual Insurance*	53	78	First National Bank-Lyons	349	583
First National Bank-Lyons	8	9	First National Bank-Lyons	51	77	Packers Bank and Trust	345	587
Valmont Industries	7	13	Bank of Norfolk	51	78	Crete Carrier	344	577
Guarantee Mutual Life	7	9	Crete Carrier	50	72	Farmers Mutual Insurance	287	534
Farmers State Bank-Aurora	6	8	Guarantee Mutual Life	47	68	Farmers State Bank-Aurora	279	478
Crete Carrier	6	8	Farmers State Bank-Aurora	47	68	First National Bank-Wisner	270	461
Majers Corp.	6	6	First United Bank-Neligh	46	65	First United Bank-Neligh	270	461
Union Bank and Trust	5	5	First National Bank-Wisner	46	64	Bank of Papillion	270	461
Farmers State Bk-Lexington	5	5	Farmers State Bk-Lexington	46	65	Farmers State Bk-Lexington	247	519
First National Bank-Wisner	5	6	Bank of Papillion	44	64	ConAgra	247	491
First United Bank-Neligh	5	5	Woodmen Accident & Life*	44	65	Peter Kiewit	247	464
Bank of Papillion	5	5	ConAgra	43	70	Berkshire Hathaway	228	506
First National of Nebraska	5	5	Majers Corp.	43	63	Woodmen Accident & Life	208	369
Harlan County Bank	5	6	Berkshire Hathaway	43	77	Norwest Bank-Nebraska	205	338
Berkshire Hathaway	5	5	Mutual of Omaha Ins. Co.*	39	57	Union Bank and Trust	187	311
Peter Kiewit	5	10	Mall Corp.*	34	49	Beatrice National Bank*	180	355
Burt County Bank	4	4	IBP*	34	50	Guarantee Mutual Life	174	306
Farmers/Merchants-Bloomfield	4	4	Nebraska Boiler	33	50	Pegler-Sysco Food*	172	339
Washington Bank	4	4	Norwest Bank-Nebraska	32	52	Security Mutual Life	172	304
Security Mutual Life	4	7	Nebraska Farmer*	31	49	Dutton-Lainson*		
ConAgra	4	10	ISCO*	30	44			
Nebraska Boiler	4	4	Harris Technology*	30	44			
American Charter S&L	4	4	Great Plains Natural Gas*	30	44			
Data Transmission	4	4	Durham Resources*	30	44			

*Corporations not ranked in prior columns

61

Table 3.3 Social fabric matrix of Nebraska central core director deliveries, 1988-89

RECEIVING CORPORATIONS → / DELIVERING CORPORATIONS ↓	(1)	(2)	(3)	(4)	(5)	(6)	(7)	(8)	(9)	(10)	(11)	(12)	(13)	(14)	(15)	(16)	(17)
(1) FirsTier Financial			D		2D	D	4D		2D	D	3D	2D	3D	2D		10	21
(2) Norwest Nebraska			D			3D										2	4
(3) First Commerce BancShares	D	D			D			4D					D	2D		6	10
(4) Union Bank & Trust															2D	1	2
(5) Ameritas Life	2D		D						D					4D	D	5	9
(6) Guarantee Mutual	D	3D														2	4
(7) Woodmen Acc. & Life	4D													2D		2	6
(8) Security Mutual			4D		D											2	5
(9) Farmers Mutual	2D				D									D		3	4
(10) Berkshire Hathaway	D										D	D	D			4	4
(11) ConAgra	3D									D		3D	3D			4	10
(12) Peter Kiewit	2D									D	3D		3D			4	9
(13) Valmont	3D		D						D	D	3D	3D				6	12
(14) Lincoln Telecommunications	2D		2D		4D		2D	D	D				D		D	8	14
(15) Crete Carrier				2D										D		3	4
(16) TOTAL ENTRIES	10	2	6	1	5	2	2	2	3	4	4	4	6	8	3		
(17) COLUMN TOTALS	21	4	10	2	9	4	6	5	4	4	10	9	12	14	4		

Figure 3.3 Social fabric digraph of the Nebraska central planning core director deliveries, 1988-89

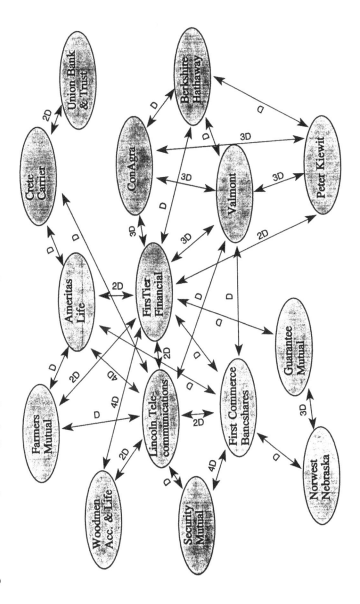

corporations as the Nebraska Central Planning Core Corporations (NCPC), consistent with the term used earlier by Munkirs (1985). Table 3.3 is a SFM that indicates the number of directors being delivered by NCPC corporations to other NCPC corporations. The digraph for Table 3.3 is contained in Figure 3.3. Each edge (line) in Figure 3.3 represents a cell in Table 3.3, indicating the number of directors from the corresponding cell in Figure 3.3.

THE NCPC/NU SOCIAL FABRIC MATRIX

Because of the strong interest in technology policy and in who controls technology research in universities, the relationship between the CPC corporate directors and the University of Nebraska (NU) has also been researched. NU is Nebraska's land grant university system and the major university research centre for the state of Nebraska.

To outline the extent of such overlap, NU is added to the SFM of the NCPC found in Table 3.3 above. The new SFM with NU included is found in Table 3.4, with the digraph expressing the matrix in Figure 3.4.

The delivery entries in Table 3.4 are the same as in Table 3.3 except for the NU system, added as row 16 and column 16. The entries in row 16 are the deliveries made by NU to the NCPC corporations; in column 16 the entries are the deliveries made from the NCPC corporations to NU. The deliveries from NU to the corporations are designated by U, which indicates that those persons are in an important decision-making position at the university. They all serve in two capacities: as a university official and as a corporate director.

These entries are displayed in Figure 3.4, a digraph which indicates the number of UDs (a UD being a person who is both a NU official and a NCPC corporate director). By adding NU to the NCPC matrix and digraph, the substantial degree to which the University is connected with the 15 core corporations, and the extent of their director deliveries, become clear. NU has more primary translocks than any other corporation in the matrix: there are 37 corporate officials involved in 11 primary translocks. In comparison, FirsTier, as the highest ranking corporation in primary translocks, has fewer than NU, FirsTier having 32 officials involved in 11 primary translocks. The highest number of primary locks between any two institutions occurs between FirsTier and NU. These number 11. Excluding the University, the greatest number of PCTs between two corporations is 4. Of the 15 corporations that comprise the NCPC, 73 per cent deliver at least 1 director to NU. The

Figure 3.4   Social fabric digraph of the Nebraska central planning core director deliveries to include the University of Nebraska, 1988-89

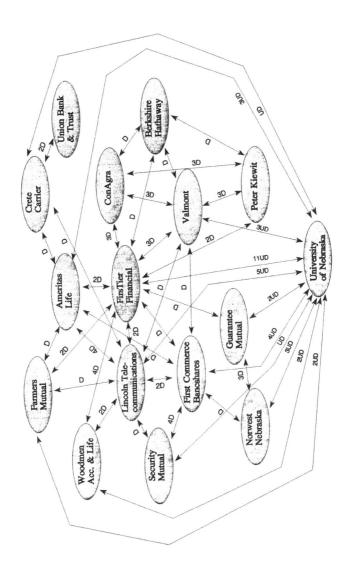

Table 3.4 *Social fabric matrix of Nebraska central planning core director deliveries to include the University of Nebraska, 1988-89*

DELIVERING CORPORATIONS \ RECEIVING CORPORATIONS	(1)	(2)	(3)	(4)	(5)	(6)	(7)	(8)	(9)	(10)	(11)	(12)	(13)	(14)	(15)	(16)	(17)	(18)
(1) FirsTier Financial			D		2D	·D	4D		2D	D	3D	2D	3D	2D		11D	11	32
(2) Norwest Nebraska			D			3D										3D	3	7
(3) First Commerce Bancshares	D	D			D			4D					D	2D		4D	7	14
(4) Union Bank & Trust															2D		1	2
(5) Ameritas Life	2D		D						D					4D	D	3D	6	12
(6) Guarantee Mutual	D	3D														2D	3	6
(7) Woodmen Acc. & Life	4D													2D		2D	3	8
(8) Security Mutual			4D						D							D	3	6
(9) Farmers Mutual	2D				D									D		2D	4	6
(10) Berkshire Hathaway	D										D	D	D				4	4
(11) ConAgra	3D									D		3D	3D				4	10
(12) Peter Kiewit	2D									D	3D		3D				4	9
(13) Valmont	3D		D							D	3D	3D		D		3D	7	15
(14) Lincoln Telecommunications	2D		2D		4D		2D		D				D		D	5D	9	19
(15) Crete Carrier				2D	D									D		D	4	5
(16) University of NE	11U	3U	4U		3U	2U	2U	U	2U				3U	5U	U		11	37
(17) TOTAL ENTRIES	11	3	7	1	6	3	3	3	4	4	4	4	7	9	4	11		
(18) COLUMN TOTALS	32	7	14	2	12	6	8	6	6	4	10	9	15	19	5	37		

66

NCPC also provides almost 50 per cent of the directors to the University of Nebraska Foundation Board of Directors, and holds 50 per cent of the foundation committee chairships.

CORPORATE OVERLAP AND TECHNOLOGY RESEARCH

As universities in the United States have become more closely linked to corporations in the areas of research and technological innovation, concern has grown with regard to conflicts of interest for faculty members, to loss of academic freedom, and to unfair advantages given to particular corporations in commercialising the results of research paid for by taxpayers. In a recent study completed by the US General Accounting Office (GAO), 35 US universities were surveyed in an attempt to assess the overall relationship between universities and business (GAO, 1992).

The GAO found that most universities have substantially expanded their technology licensing programmes since 1980, and that 73 per cent of the licence income received by the 35 universities was financed in whole or in part with federal government funding (GAO, 1992, pp. 11-12). Yet, despite the growing importance of licensing technology to corporations, many of the universities surveyed 'continue to require only voluntary disclosure by faculty and administrators' (GAO, 1992, p. 3)

Such a system of voluntary disclosure invites abuse of government funds and inappropriate access to research. 'Such inappropriate access could result from a financial or personal relationship between the business and a member of the university; or a financial relationship between the business and the university itself such as through an industrial liaison program' (GAO, 1992, p. 2).

Relationships between licensees and universities have led to conflicts of interest, as demonstrated by the following two GAO findings.

The 35 universities reported that: (1) scientists who developed the technologies for 61 of the exclusive licences consulted for owned a substantial amount of stock in, or had other relationships with, the licensees; and (2) members of industrial liaison programmes were granted exclusive licences in four cases. In 12 additional cases, companies that had long-term agreements with universities to fund general research received exclusive licenses for technologies they did not directly co-sponsor (GAO, 1992, p. 3).

Eighteen universities, including 14 with foreign members, also reported that industrial liaison programme members can get access to the results of federally-funded research before those results are made publicly available to others, including to US companies that are not programme members (GAO, 1992, p. 4).

The GAO studied universities all across the nation without attempting to determine whether any were connected with the regional or national CPC. Upon studying two recent technology research projects for the University of Nebraska, it was discovered that both involve Nebraska CPC members.

One is a University of Nebraska research and technology park that is being developed by a coalition of six corporations and the University of Nebraska Foundation. NCPC members are playing a prominent role in its development. The most prominent man on the NCPC (whose wife and son-in-law also serve on the NCPC) is the major developer of the project. The development will cover 550 acres and is to include a shopping centre, office buildings, light industry and a golf course, in addition to the research park and technology core. The mayor of the city sought a proposal from the coalition rather than sell the 550 acres to any other interested developer.

The second research project that involves NCPC institutions (to include the University of Nebraska) as well as Nebraska technology firms is referred to as EPSCoR (Experimental Program to Stimulate Competitive Research). Its purpose is to set research priorities and become more successful in obtaining government research funds for higher education that will be beneficial for the commercial efforts of private corporations. EPSCoR is governed by a committee appointed by the Governor of Nebraska. The committee includes members from higher education institutions, corporations as well as one member from the Office of the Governor. According to the proposal, 'all personnel involved in the Nebraska EPSCoR program will be responsible to the Committee. All proposals and reports to the Environmental Protection Agency or other Federal agencies will be by or through the Committee' (EPSCoR Project, 1991, p. 15).

EPSCoR is crafted to provide a state planning and evaluation process for research. 'It will yield a true public-private partnership that will have a greater industry involvement, (and) will have a greater potential for good research and technology transfer ...' (EPSCoR Project, 1992a, p. 3). The main idea behind the establishment of EPSCoR was to acquire 'funding support that would have a high probability for technology transfer to industry in Nebraska' (EPSCoR Project, 1992a, p. 2).

The proposal to the federal government states clearly that EPSCoR is to allow corporations to be involved in establishing goals, priorities and criteria for evaluating Nebraska research projects (EPSCoR Project, 1992b, p. 2). In addition, private corporations are to have a lead in determining what kind of research is to be pursued, while commercialisation is to be determined by EPSCoR without input from legislative bodies, taxpayers or faculty groups. EPSCoR is to be a strong catalyst for increasing the linkage between universities and corporations. 'The objective of this new linkage is to foster fundamental and strategic research which can in turn stimulate knowledge and technology transfer among the various universities and colleges, foster creative collaborations with the private sector, and build a critical mass of research strengths ...' (EPSCoR Project, 1992b, p. 1).

Although research decisions are to be made without the input of legislative bodies that represent the taxpayers, the latter will provide 75 percent of the funds for research. Private corporations have promised to raise the remaining 25 per cent. Contributing corporations will include firms which collaborate with university scientists as well as engineers whose research proposals are to be included (EPSCoR Project, 1992a, p. 12).

This evidence indicates that universities in the US are allowing their research and technological innovations to be directed more and more by corporations. In addition, it indicates that in the Nebraska case, that leadership is provided by collaborating NCPC members. Thus, in order to understand the research infrastructure and technological development, future research on corporate organisational overlaps should include universities as part of the corporate system.

CORPORATE REACHABILITY

To extend the analysis, structural modelling techniques developed in anthropology and sociology are used to assist in analysing and learning more about corporate networks, thereby furthering our ability to describe, understand and provide an analytical consistency sufficient for policy making. These techniques and matrix manipulations have been used for a broad range of analysis: anthropological analysis of caste food transactions in India; the sociological analysis of the personal communication network for family planning information in Africa; the political ties among elite cliques in the United States, to mention a few examples. Using structuralist techniques, it is possible to determine numerous structural relationships after basic social information is organised in the social fabric matrix. These relationships include reachability, proximity, linkage distance, cliques, clusters, centrality, interest groups, power blocs,and so forth.[3]

Reachability Matrix

Harary, Norman and Cartwright (1965) define a path from node A to node B (corporation A to B) as reachable if there exists a sequence of deliveries or paths from node A to B. The reachability matrix shows whether a path exists by which a specific corporation can reach or pass information and knowledge to another (see Hayden and Stephenson (1993) for the mechanics of computing a reachability matrix). A reachability matrix provides useful structural information regarding a system of corporate directorships. In a large network of real-world corporations, identifying a system of reachable corporations is difficult without the assistance of a reachability matrix which will show which groups of corporations are connected or reachable to each other through their respective boards of directors.[4]

As stated earlier, for the 100 Nebraska corporations with at least one PCT, a 100 x 100 reachability matrix was created for the network of corporate directorships. The rows and columns of the reachability matrix can be rearranged through a common algorithm to show the connected blocs down the diagonal (Warfield, 1976). Six groups of corporations are shown in Table 3.5.

Table 3.5 Nebraska groups of reachable corporations

Group 1. A group of 84 corporations. This group includes Nebraska's CPC as well as FirsTier Financial, ConAgra, Berkshire Hathaway, Ameritas Life, and Valmont Industries.

Group 2. A group of 7 corporations consisting of First National Bank of Nebraska, First National Bank and Trust of Columbus, Burt County State Bank, Harlan County Bank, Farmers and Merchants Bank of Bloomfield, Washington County Bank, and Nebraska Public Power District.

Group 3. A group of 3 corporations: Abbott Bank Group, Lockwood Corporation, and First State Bank of Scottsbluff.

Group 4. A group of 2 corporations: Mid City Bank and Mutual Protective Insurance.

Group 5. A group of 2 corporations: Hastings State Bank and Havelock Bank.

Group 6. A group of 2 corporations: Vistar Bank and Miller and Paine.

Table 3.5 identifies the corporations included in each group. The large group of 84 includes the Nebraska CPC. FirsTier Financial is one of these corporations. Inspecting the FirsTier row of a reachability matrix would reveal that the row contains 83 '1's (there would be no '1' in the FirsTier x FirsTier cell). That is, FirsTier has reachability to all the corporations in Group 1. Note that three out of the six groups contain only two corporations. The corporations in each of these three groups can share information through directorships with only one other corporation. We are able to determine with this technique that not all the corporate world is reachable through corporate directorship exchange within the state of Nebraska. Others, for example Gardiner Means (1939), did not determine these kinds of divisions.

As indicated in Hayden and Stephenson (1992), the University of Nebraska is closely tied to FirsTier Financial and Nebraska's CPC. Adding the University of Nebraska to the matrix extends the reachability of the entire corporate directorship system in two ways. First, the University is connected with seven corporations previously not delivering even one director to the original list of 100 corporations. Thus the SFM including the University is expanded in size to 108 x 108; the university plus seven additional corporations. Second, the University ties together corporations from previously disconnected groups. For example, Vistar Bank and FirsTier both deliver a director(s) to the University Foundation. Thus Vistar and Miller and Paine (Group 6) can now 'reach' the original group of 84 corporations through University Foundation Board meetings. The largest group of 84 corporations is now expanded to 94 organisations - 93 corporations (7 new corporations, Vistar, and Miller and Paine) plus NU. The University, however, does not tie together all the previously disconnected groups listed in Table 3.5. The second big-bank group (Group 2), headed by First National Bank of Nebraska, has no linkages to NU. Of interest for future research is the fact that First National does not serve as a financial agent for NU while FirsTier does in several capacities.

Path Distance Matrix

Graph theory provides another potentially useful matrix, known as a path distance or simply distance matrix (Burt, 1982). A distance matrix is closely related to a reachability matrix and is built using geodesic measures. Harary *et al.* (1965) define a geodesic as the minimum length path between A and B. A distance matrix shows the geodesic distances between corporations. Consistent with our interests, this technique can be utilised to determine how closely corporations are linked, and whether the linkage is through PCTs, SCTs or TCTs. It should be stressed, however, that a geodesic measure does not reveal the degree to which corporations share overlapping sets of directorships.[5]

A distance matrix for Nebraska corporate directorships was computed. The distance matrix reveals that 30 corporations have representatives sitting on FirsTier's board. Or, stated differently, FirsTier meets 30 other corporations on a primary (PCT) basis. In addition, FirsTier meets representatives from an additional 29 corporations on other corporate boards through secondary connections and another 17 corporations on a tertiary basis. The FirsTier row in a path distance matrix would contain 30 'Is' (PCTs) 29 'Zs' (SCTs) and 17 '3s' (TCTs). See Hayden and Stephenson (1993).

Through regular corporate board meetings, Firstier officers and directors come in face-to-face contact with officers/directors of 59 other Nebraska corporations (primary and secondary connections), or 71 per cent of the other 83 corporations in the Group 1 network. In addition, 14 of the 15 core corporations reach at least 70 per cent of the 84 corporations through their primary, secondary and tertiary connections. When the University of Nebraska is included in the path distance matrix (see Hayden and Stephenson, 1993), then the results demonstrate that the University is heavily tied to the Nebraska CPC, so much so that NU is an important centre of corporate translocks. As illustrated in Table 3.6, 40 corporations (or 43 per cent of the 94 organisations now in group 1) are represented on important NU decision-making groups through primary connections. In addition, NU representatives meet 87 per cent of the Group 1 corporations on a face-to-face basis through either primary or secondary translocks.

Since the university is heavily tied to the corporate sector, NU also shortens the 'distances' between corporations. For instance, if we count only corporate ties, Farmers Mutual can reach Crete Carrier only on a tertiary basis. If the University is taken into consideration, however, Farmers Mutual and Crete Carrier officers and directors now meet face-to-face on the University Foundation board.

CORPORATE CENTRALITY MEASURES

An early concept of centrality was applied by Bavelas (1948) in a study of human communication. Since that time, sociology and anthropology have made substantial contributions to further develop the concept of centrality. The applications of centrality have ranged from the study of political integration in India to investigations of twelfth-century river transportation in Russia (Freeman, 1979) and to the study of human communication networks through interlocking boards of directorships (Sonquist and Koenig, 1975; Mizruchi, 1982; Mintz and Schwartz, 1985).[6] Although there are different measures of centrality, as Freeman

(1979, p. 217) states, 'everyone agrees, it seems, that centrality is an important structural attribute of social networks'.

Table 3.6 Minimum distances between Nebraska CPC corporations and University of Nebraska that can be reached on a primary, secondary and tertiary basis

	Primary		Secondary		Tertiary	
1. FirsTier Financial	31	(33%)	42	(79%)	19	(99%)
2. Lincoln Telecom	16	(17%)	55	(76%)	17	(95%)
3. First National Commerce	15	(16%)	55	(75%)	17	(94%)
4. Ameritas Life	12	(13%)	58	(75%)	18	(95%)
5. Crete Carrier Corp.	7	(8%)	43	(54%)	34	(90%)
6. Valmont Industries	8	(9%)	53	(66%)	25	(92%)
7. Farmers Mutual Life	4	(4%)	54	(62%)	30	(95%)
8. Union Bank	5	(5%)	7	(13%)	43	(59%)
9. Peter Kiewit	5	(5%)	28	(35%)	40	(78%)
10. Berkshire Hathaway	5	(5%)	28	(35%)	40	(78%)
11. ConAgra	4	(4%)	28	(34%)	40	(77%)
12. Woodmen Acc. and Life	4	(4%)	52	(60%)	31	(94%)
13. Norwest Bank—Nebraska	10	(11%)	49	(63%)	31	(97%)
14. Security Mutual Ins.	5	(5%)	45	(54%)	33	(89%)
15. Guarantee Mutual Ins.	8	(9%)	56	(69%)	24	(95%)
16. University of Nebraska	40	(43%)	41	(87%)	8	(96%)

* The numbers in parenthesis are cumulative percentages based on the 94 organisations in Group 1.

Geodesic-based Centrality Measures

Freeman (1979) has made important conceptual clarifications to the concept of centrality. Classifying thirty years of research, he identifies three distinct centrality concepts: degree, betweenness and closeness.[7] Each measure reveals different structural properties associated with an actor's (corporation's) position within a social network.

Degree Centrality: The degree of a node (for example a corporation) is 'simply the count of the number of other points that are adjacent to it and with which it is, therefore, in direct contact' (Freeman, 1979, p. 219). The degree of a corporate node is simply the number of PCTs held by a given corporation. A corporation with the largest number of PCTs is in some respects a focus of communication activity since that corporation is in direct contact with a larger number of corporations than any other. The larger the number of direct contacts, the more central the corporation is in the network. Freeman views degree as an important index of potential communication activity.

Betweenness Centrality: A second view of centrality is based on betweenness. Freeman (1979) defines betweenness as the frequency with which a point falls between pairs of other points on the shortest or geodesic paths connecting them. A corporation is central to the extent to which it is located on paths linking pairs of other corporations.[8] Freeman calls betweenness an index of the potential control of communication by an actor.

Closeness Centrality: The third geodesic centrality measure, closeness, is based on how close a point or corporation is to all other points in the network. The closeness of a point is the sum of the lengths of the shortest paths (geodesics) between one point and all other points of a connected graph. Freeman (1979) points out that the closeness measure can impact on a communication network in two different ways. First, a corporation is 'viewed as central to the extent it can avoid the control potential of others' (Freeman, 1979, p. 224). A non-central corporation is more likely to send and receive information through others, and therefore is dependent on intermediaries. According to Freeman (1979), this sense of the closeness measure is an index of communication independence. The second interpretation of a closeness-based centrality measure originated with Bavelas (1948). A central position in a network shows that a message or directive originating in a central position would spread through the network in less time than a message sent from a peripheral node. Freeman (1979, p. 225) describes this idea as 'shorter distances mean fewer message transmissions, shorter times and lower costs'. The second interpretation of a closeness-based centrality measure has been described as an index of communication efficiency. These interpretations are more suggestive than definitive since the closeness centrality concept extends beyond simply speed or efficiency.

Sabidussi (1966) proposed a straightforward technique to calculate a closeness measure of centrality. The closeness of any point is calculated by summing the geodesic distances from one corporation (point) to all other points. In short, this closeness measure is just the sum of a row or column in a path distance matrix. Thus the lower the closeness centrality score, the higher the centrality (for details see Hayden and Stephenson,

1993).

All three centrality measures that Freeman identifies are based on geodesic measures. By using such measures, an assumption is made that information or influence is always transmitted through the shortest possible path. Thus reachable, but nongeodesic, pathways are assumed never to be used. Therefore, geodesic measures fail to account for system concepts of redundancy and equifinality.

Correlative Measure of Centrality

Bonacich (1972) developed a widely used measure of centrality based on patterns of overlapping memberships.[9] This technique is a standard way to compute centrality for interlocking directorate research (Bonacich, 1987; Mariolis, 1975; Mizruchi, 1982; Caswell, 1987).

> Overlap with central groups (whose members in turn belong to many groups) contributes more to the centrality of a group than overlap with isolated groups. Overlap with a central group gives access to a greater number of powerful individuals, whereas overlap with relatively isolated groups gives access to relatively few. The number of overlaps with other groups alone does not involve such a weighing (Bonacich, 1972, p. 177).

The Bonacich measure of centrality can be defined as the summed connections to others, weighted by their centralities (Bonacich, 1987). The summed connections are the number of PCTs between corporations, adjusted by the number of members on each board (see Appendix 3.2 for details). These connections are similar to correlation coefficients between corporate boards and range in value from 0 to 1. A zero coefficient would indicate no PCT overlap between two corporations. A coefficient of 1 would indicate that every member of one corporation is also a board member of the second corporation. A system of simultaneous equations is then solved (one for each corporation in the network) to arrive at a vector of centrality weights. The centrality measure is the eigenvector associated with the largest characteristic eigenvalue. This calculation is similar to that done in factor analysis. Bonacich's measure is different from the other centrality measures because it does not rely on the structural properties of graphs to generate a centrality score. However, Stephenson and Zelen (1989, p. 4) point out that Bonacich's approach 'neglects multiple share paths between points in a network'.

Redundancy Measure of Centrality

Stephenson and Zelen (1989) have recently pointed out some of the potential limitations associated with Freeman's geodesic-based centrality measures. Freeman's measures assume that communication occurs only on the shortest possible distance from one point to another. Like Bonacich, Stephenson and Zelen point out that these measures ignore reachable, but nongeodesic, communication pathways. These authors have thus proposed a centrality measure based on all possible reachable pathways. Unlike Bonacich's centrality measure, the Stephenson and Zelen approach takes into account multiple shared deliveries between corporations. Stephenson and Zelen implicitly acknowledge the importance of redundancy in a system.

The corporation which carries the greatest amount of 'information' from all paths is the most central corporation in the network. As Stephenson and Zelen (1989, p. 8) state, 'generally the information is inversely proportionate to the distance of a path, and the information in a combined path is equal to the sum of the information of the individual paths'. Stephenson and Zelen's measure has additional advantages over other centrality measures. First, it captures the system's concept of redundancy which geodesic measures ignore. Second, Stephenson and Zelen's measure explicitly acknowledges the weighing system inherent in all centrality measures. Thus their method also allows the weighing schemes to be inspected and defined by the researcher. There appears to be no sound theoretical justification regarding a weighing of paths or path messages; this continues to be a weakness and point of criticism of all centrality measures.[10]

Comparing Different Centrality Measures for Nebraska Corporations

Each of these five measures are now used to rank the most central corporations for the Nebraska corporate network. The ranking from the five centrality measures are compared with Hayden and Stephenson's (1992) original listing of the most central corporations. The centrality ordering from the five measures are listed in Table 3.7, with bold type denoting NCPC corporations as determined in the original 1992 study. The absolute centralisation scores are located in Table 3.8.

In comparing the different centrality measures, it is evident that the overlap and redundancy-based centrality measures of Bonacich and Stephenson-Zelen generate the same listing of central corporations as that of Hayden and Stephenson. The ordering of the two overlap centrality measures, however, differed slightly from the original listing. For instance, the Stephenson and Zelen centrality measures both ranked Norwest and Guarantee Mutual higher than did either Bonacich or Hayden and Stephenson. These two corporations each had a relatively large number of primary corporate translocks, but a majority of these were with peripheral corporations. This means that the Bonacich rankings, as those of Hayden and Stephenson, placed greater importance on overlaps with more central corporations.

Table 3.7 Comparison of centrality rankings for Nebraska's CPC (without NU)

HAYDEN & STEPHENSON	DEGREE	BETWEEN-NESS	CLOSE-NESS	CORRELA-TIVE	REDUNDANCY
1. FirsTier	**FirsTier**	**FirsTier**	**FirsTier**	**FirsTier**	**FirsTier**
2. LTT	**LTT**	**FCB**	**FCB**	**LTT**	**LTT**
3. FCB	**FCB**	**Norwest**	**LTT**	**Ameritas**	**FCB**
4. Ameritas	**Ameritas**	**LTT**	**Ameritas**	**FCB**	**Ameritas**
5. Crete	**Norwest**	**Ameritas**	**Valmont**	**Valmont**	**Norwest**
6. Valmont	**Guarantee**	**Guarantee**	**Norwest**	**Crete**	**Valmont**
7. Farmers M	**Valmont**	Millard L	**Guarantee**	**Farmers**	**Crete C**
8. Union B	**Crete**	Mutual O	Mutual O	**Berkshire**	**Guarantee**
9. Kiewit	**Union B**	ChiefAuto	**Farmers M**	**Kiewit**	**Berkshire**
10. Berkshire	**Berkshire**	Lozier	**Woodmen**	**ConAgra**	**Kiewit**
11. ConAgra	**Kiewit**	Cons Save	Cont Inse	**Woodmen**	**Union**
12. Woodmen	Amer C	NP Dodge	**Berkshire**	**Union**	**Farmers M**
13. Norwest	**Security**	**Security**	**Kiewit**	**Guarantee**	**ConAgra**
14. Security	**ConAgra**	Centerra	**ConAgra**	**Norwest**	**Woodmen**
15. Guarantee	Data T	**Valmont**	Mall Corp		**Security M**

Bold print indicates the corporations which also appear in the original 1992 ranking.

Freeman's closeness and betweenness centrality scores showed the greatest deviation from the original listing. The closeness centrality ranked Mutual of Omaha Insurance eighth in overall centrality, whereas

Dynamics of the firm

Mutual of Omaha failed to make the list of top 15 corporations in the overlap measures. Thus, while Mutual of Omaha directorship translocks were not extensively overlapping, their directors were located so as to reach a large number of corporations through a minimum of steps.

Table 3.8 Scores for five of the centrality measures (without NU)

DEGREE		BETWEENNESS		CLOSENESS		CORRELATIVE		REDUNDANCY	
FirsTier	30	FirsTier	2002	FirsTier	173	FirsTier	.48	FirsTier	.98
LTT	15	FCB	980	FCB	189	LTT	.34	LTT	.94
FCB	14	Norwest	732	LTT	195	Ameritas	.28	FCB	.93
Ameritas	11	LTT	513	Ameritas	200	NBC	.25	Ameritas	.90
Norwest	9	Ameritas	461	Valmont	213	Valmont	.20	Norwest	.86
Guarantee	7	Guarantee	441	Norwest	218	Crete	.17	Valmont	.86
Valmont	7	Millard L	316	Guarantee	219	Farmers M	.15	Crete	.81
Crete	6	Mutual O	306	Mutual O	227	Berkshire	.13	Guarantee	.80
Union Bk	5	ChiefAuto	289	Farmers M	223	Kiewit	.13	Berkshire	.77
Berkshire	5	Lozier	250	Woodmen	236	ConAgra	.12	Kiewit	.77
Kiewit	5	Cons Save	163	Cont Ins	249	Woodmen	.12	Union Bk	.76
Amer C	4	NP Dodge	162	Berkshire	249	Union Bk	.10	Farmers M	.76
Security	4	Security	130	Kiewit	249	Guarantee	.10	ConAgra	.76
ConAgra	4	Centerra	87	ConAgra	249	Norwest	.09	Woodmen	.72
Data T	4	Valmont	86	Mall Corp	252			Security	.71

The betweenness centrality scores perhaps yielded the most surprising results. After the first five corporations, Freeman's betweenness centrality ranking had little in common with the other centrality measures. Apparently the first five corporations accounted for most of the 'betweenness' in the core set of corporations. For instance, ConAgra had a zero betweenness centrality score. Since its geodesic did not lead towards even one other corporation. On the other hand, quite peripheral corporations, such as Millard Lumber, attained a relatively high score because they stood on geodesics linking core firms and even more peripheral firms.

The centrality measures were also recalculated with the University included in the network. The results are presented in Table 3.9. All the centrality measures ranked the University as the most central organisation in the network. The presence of the University also impacted on the centrality scores of each corporation. Large national corporations, such as ConAgra and Peter Kiewit, no longer ranked in the top 15 corporations according to the Bonacich correlative centrality measure. These national corporations were not directly tied to the University. Smaller, regional corporations such as Durham Resources, had direct ties with NU and through this association boosted their centrality within the network.

Network Centrality

Up to this point, only centralities of specific nodes or corporations have been discussed. The centrality concepts, however, have also been proposed as useful in measuring the centrality of the entire network or system. Freeman (1979) points out that there are two commonly held notions regarding network centrality which have emerged in the literature, one interpretation being related to graph compactness. This view of network centrality uses a graph to show the degree of closeness between points. For a 5 x 5 network, each of the five corporations in the most central network would share a director with every other corporation. The graph would be completely connected and would have maximum compactness; thus the digraph for this kind of matrix exhibits a non-hierarchical structure since no one node is more central than any other node.

An alternative view, according to Freeman, arises out of research on communication in social networks. As Freeman states, 'from this perspective the centrality of an entire network should index the tendency of a single point to be more central than all other points in the network' (Freeman, 1979, p. 227). Freeman calls this an index of the centralisation for the network. Endorsing this view, Leavitt (1951) argued that problem-solving ability in a social network is related to the tendency of one point to dominate the most central position. For a 5 x 5 network, the network exhibiting the greatest centrality would have four corporations sharing directors only with the fifth corporation.

Freeman concludes that the latter interpretation is the more appropriate way to think of network centrality. He developed three network centralisation measures that correspond with the degree, closeness and between point centrality measures discussed earlier. (See Appendix 3.2 for details.) Each of Freeman's network centralisation indices measures the amount to which the centrality of the most central point exceeds the centrality of all other points and is 'expressed as a ratio of that excess to its maximum possible value for a graph containing the observed number of points' (Freeman, 1979, p. 227).

Table 3.9 Scores for five of the centrality measures (with NU)

DEGREE		BETWEENNESS		CLOSENESS		CORRELATIVE		REDUNDANCY	
NU	**40**	NU	**2205**	NU	**160**	NU	**.47**	NU	**1.3**
FirsTier	31	FirsTier	1491	FirsTier	176	FirsTier	.37	FirsTier	1.3
LTT	16	FCB	580	LTT	197	LTT	.29	LTT	1.2
FCB	15	Guarantee	491	FCB	198	Ameritas	.24	FCB	1.2
Ameritas	12	Ameritas	349	Ameritas	202	FCB	.22	Ameritas	1.2
Norwest	10	LTT	315	Guarantee	212	Valmont	.17	Norwest	1.1
Guarantee	8	Mutual O	277	Norwest	213	Crete	.17	Valmont	1.1
Valmont	8	Cons Save	183	Valmont	216	Farmers M	.14	Crete C	1.1
Crete C	7	Security	163	Farmers M	222	Woodmen	.13	Guarantee	1.0
Union Bk	5	Occ Saving	92	Woodmen	225	Norwest	.12	Farmers M	1.0
Berkshire	5	Vistar	92	Mall Corp	228	Guarantee	.11	Woodmen	.98
Kiewit	5	Data Trans	92	Durham R	230	Security	.10	Union Bk	.97
Security	5	NP Dodge	83	GP Gas	230	Durham R	.10	Berkshire	.97
Amer C	5	ChiefAuto	67	Crete C	234	GPN Gas	.10	Kiewit	.97
ConAgra	4	Valmont	67	Security	237	Info Tech	.10	Security	.96
Data Trans	4	Amer Char	41	Scoular	243			ConAgra	.93
FarmersM	4								
Woodmen	4								
Mall Corp	4								
NP Dodge	4								

Freeman's network centrality concept was used to calculate degree, closeness and betweenness network centralisation indexes for Nebraska corporate directorships. Overall network centrality for the four measures was calculated with and without the University of Nebraska in order to determine how the University influences the centrality of the whole network. The results in Hayden and Stephenson (1993) show that the University of Nebraska increases the centralisation index for two of the three network centrality measures. The degree and closeness indexes increased when the University was added to the data base. Only the betweenness centralisation index decreased when the University was added. Like the individual corporate centrality measures, the betweenness centralisation index results differed substantially from all other centrality measures.

MEANING IN A SOCIAL CONTEXT

For these techniques to assist analysis, investigators need to be knowledgeable about the contextual meaning and substance of the nodes, edges, matrices, linkages and techniques. There is no network mathematics to indicate the fact that the gender of a node, for example, transforms the amount of the flow of care along a link. The boolean mathematics of a corporate network does not provide for power. Rather, is the rules of the social system represented in the network which determine the presence of power. As has been learned from recent studies that trace the communicability of the AIDS disease, a prostitute may hold a central position, have numerous linkages and reachability throughout a small town, yet no one has suggested that the centrality of a small-town prostitute provides her with power. The social rules do not allow this. By the rule of law, however, corporate directors have the power to govern. Thus, the centrality and reachability of their linkages determine the concentration, proximity and direction of power. Stinchcombe (1990) has stated that, 'potential power and actual power are the same thing and are the network phenomenon itself'.

The meaning of the network depends on what is being delivered or flowing through the network. When it is the governing directors (who carry with them the knowledge, plans and decision-making power of all their overlapping corporations) that are being delivered, real decision-making power is being concentrated when centralisation occurs. The meaning of the delivery flow is determined 'by what the people or organisations who constitute the nodes of the network do to the flow to transform it as it impinges on them, what their interpretation is of the flow for their personal situation, what conditions there are in the environment of the link (or the people in it), and what changes are going on under those conditions' (Stinchcombe, 1990, p. 130). With regard to translocking boards, an immense body of substantive knowledge has been known for decades. But only structural techniques will allow us to describe and define the system as a whole, and also measure those practices which have caused long standing social policy concerns.

POLICY PROTOCOL

Too much space in the literature has been devoted to arguments about which of these measures is the correct one. The measures differ, however, and therefore are appropriate for different purposes, situations and contexts. Some of these structural measures are now discussed in order to design provisional procedures for the purpose of implementing a policy protocol.

The policy protocol below is based on the argument that some of the structural measures developed above are relevant for determining the distribution and use of power in shaping the sociopolitical system. This broadened approach to inquiry is consistent with concerns about the social control of industry as defined by Liebhafsky (1971). The sociopolitical objections to the centralisation of the corporate decision-making network are a sufficient base to instigate policies to control excessive centralisation. In other words, when the decision-making power becomes more and more concentrated in one locus, there is less power in other institutions. Pitofsky (1978) wrote that 'despite the inconvenience, lack of predictability and general mess introduced into the economists' allegedly cohesive and tidy world of microeconomic analyses, an antitrust policy that failed to take political concerns into account would be unresponsive to the will of Congress and out of touch with the rough political consensus that has supported antitrust enforcement for almost 100 years'.

PROCEDURES FOR A CORPORATE POLICY PROTOCOL

The following five procedures are recommended as a provisional policy protocol to structure the debate concerning the legislation that will be necessary, and to provide an administrative protocol for implementing a corporate centrality and reachability policy.

The first procedure regarding centrality is to judge whether a system as a whole has become too centralised. To determine this, the Freeman network closeness centrality measure is recommended to determine how centralised the entire network is as a whole system. The closeness measure is selected because it is based on how close any one point in the system is to all other points in the network, whereas the degree and betweenness measures are more limited in their application.

Irrespective of the findings from the closeness network indicator, the second step should be to utilise the block modelling procedure provided by the reachability matrix to determine the separate groups within a system. This is analogous to clique analysis that has been widely used in the sociological literature. Means (1939) applied an early form of clique analysis to identify different corporate interest groups. Society's concern to identify subgroups has been evident for decades and now various measurement techniques are possible.

The divided system found in procedure two can be used to determine which part of the system is becoming most centralised. Thus the network closeness centrality measures selected for procedure one can be applied to each smaller group to determine in which of them the highest centralisation exists. The network closeness centrality measures selected for procedure one, coupled with the subgroup analysis in procedure two, can thus indicate if the system is becoming too centralised and what groups of corporations are at the core of such convergence.

For any corporate group that is judged to be too centralised, the third procedure is to determine which particular corporations are the most centralised within the system. To accomplish this, the Stephenson-Zelen redundancy ranking should be applied to determine which corporations have the highest centralisation coefficients. The Stephenson-Zelen redundancy or Bonacich correlative measure should be selected for two reasons. First, these two measures can account for the extent of communication overlap, whereas the Freeman centrality measures (degree, betweenness and closeness) for particular corporations are less extensive. Second, the directorship edges among corporations can be weighted by the number of directors delivered, whereas the other Freeman techniques do not allow for the weighing of different connections. The redundancy indicators for each corporation can be used to identify those requiring adjustment.

The fourth step is to identify the particular paths through which individual corporations of concern reach other corporations in order to decide which paths should be monitored or terminated. The particular sequence of paths can be determined by the path-distance matrix. A geodesic subgraph of a path-distance matrix can be used to list all corporations that one corporation goes through to reach another. Thus this tool can be used to inform corporations which director deliveries should be terminated so that their reachability can be limited to the desired level.

The fifth procedure is to determine whether corporations are using other agencies, such as the university, as a means to enhance their reachability and centralisation. This can be accomplished by completing the same procedures as outlined in steps one through four with other agencies included in the matrix. The solution is simple if the agencies are governmental such as a land grant university. Given the public purpose of government agencies and the democratic control inherent in them, the officers, directors, decision-makers and other personnel should not be allowed to serve on private corporate boards. If the agencies are not governmental, for example in the case of private foundations, they can be included as part of the corporate network and their directorships treated accordingly; they should not be allowed to overstep the degree of centralisation considered socially desirable.

Given the 'development of systematic and transferable methods for analyzing the structure of the qualities and quantities of flows among links in networks' (Stinchcombe, 1990, p. 120), it is now possible to design consistent and equitable policy procedures for achieving the desired level of corporate centralisation.

FUTURE RESEARCH

The future research agenda with regard to corporations should be to expand the matrix to include deliveries among corporations other than directors. Other deliveries which are covered in Munkirs' study of capitalist transformation include: stocks, bonds, transfer agents, trustee services, registrars, joint subsidiary ownership and so forth (Munkirs, 1985). The structural techniques outlined above can then be applied to these concerns to determine the degree of system centralisation for each, the centralisation of each corporation, as well as the patterns of reachability from corporation to corporation. The Stephenson-Zelen redundancy measurement technique should be especially useful for stock ownership because it will not only allow for the determination of the level of centralisation but, in addition, the ownership linkage can be weighted by the dollar value of the stock owned.

A great deal of scholarly interest has been generated by the industrial clusters created through subcontracting relationships. Subcontracting of the 'hollow' corporation takes place for numerous reasons: to squeeze supply, to avoid labour union contracts, to gain the cost advantages of specialisation by smaller firms, to use others' distribution services, to gain technological access, as a production planning strategy and so forth. The SFM and boolean techniques demonstrated above could serve as the next step in defining, modelling and analyzing subcontracting networks.

Centralisation techniques should also be applied to areas other than corporate concerns. The software for applying these techniques, as developed for this chapter, is now available; thus it is readily applicable to other problem areas which can be defined and articulated in the social fabric matrix. Since institutions are patterns of behaviour, structural methods explained above should allow us to more fully measure, define and refine those patterns in all areas.

APPENDIX 3.1 GLOSSARY OF ACRONYMS AND SYMBOLS

BOD	Board of Directors
CPC	Central Planning Core
CPSP	Centralised Private Sector Planning
D	Member of a Board of Directors
EPSCoR	Experimental Programme to Stimulate Competitive Research
FCB	First Commerce Bancshares
GPN Gas	Great Plains Natural Gas
LTT	Lincoln Telecommunications
NCPC	Nebraska Central Planning Core
NU	Nebraska University (Entire System)
PCT	Primary Corporate Translock
PDT	Primary Director Translock
SCT	Secondary Corporate Translock
SDT	Secondary Director Translock
TCT	Tertiary Corporate Translock
TDT	Tertiary Director Translock
U	University Decision Maker
UD	University Decision Maker who is also a Director for a Corporation
Z	A 5 x 5 adjacency matrix listed in Figure 3.5

APPENDIX 3.2 CALCULATING DIFFERENT CENTRALITY MEASURES

A) Calculating PCTs, SCTs, and TCTs Through Simple Matrix Manipulations

In terms of graph theory, the SFM is an adjacency matrix. A simple adjacency matrix, Z, representing the digraph in Figure 3.2 is shown in Figure 3.5.

Dynamics of the firm

Figure 3.5 Adjacency Matrix Z

$$
Z = \begin{array}{c} \\ \\ \\ \\ \\ \end{array}
\begin{array}{c} A \\ B \\ C \\ K \\ J \end{array}
\overset{\displaystyle A\ B\ C\ K\ J}{\left[\begin{array}{ccccc}
0 & 1 & 0 & 0 & 1 \\
1 & 0 & 1 & 0 & 1 \\
0 & 1 & 0 & 1 & 1 \\
0 & 0 & 1 & 0 & 1 \\
1 & 1 & 1 & 1 & 0
\end{array}\right]}
$$

Raising matrix Z to successive powers can be used to measure indirect relations between corporations (Luce and Perry, 1949). This is very similar, but not exactly equal, to the SCT and TCT measures. Raising an adjacency matrix to higher powers can provide a very simple way to calculate secondary and tertiary corporate translocks. For instance, squaring matrix Z from Figure 3.5 yields:

$$
Z^2 = \begin{bmatrix}
2 & 1 & 2 & 1 & 1 \\
1 & 3 & 1 & 2 & 2 \\
2 & 1 & 3 & 1 & 2 \\
1 & 2 & 1 & 2 & 1 \\
1 & 2 & 2 & 1 & 4
\end{bmatrix}
\tag{1}
$$

This shows for instance that corporation B has one two-step connection with corporation K. This is exactly equal to the SCT measure. To calculate the total SCTs for corporations in matrix Z, just add the columns (or rows) and subtract the value on the diagonal for that column. The subtracting is essentially subtracting the PCT, which was done in the Hayden and Stephenson (1992) article. To see this, consider Figure 3.6. By raising Z to the third power, tertiary translocks can also be calculated. The calculations are shown in Figure 3.7 below. This is a simple programming procedure for any software capable of handling large matrices, such as the IML software package in SAS.

Figure 3.6 Calculating secondary corporate translocks

2	1	2	1	1		
1	3	1	2	2		
2	1	3	1	2	=	Z^2
1	2	1	2	1		
1	2	2	1	4		
7	9	9	7	10	=	Sum of the columns
- 2	3	3	2	4	=	less the value of the PCTs
5	6	6	5	6	=	SCTs

Figure 3.7 Calculating tertiary corporate translocks

2	5	3	3	6		
5	4	7	3	7		
3	7	4	5	7	=	Z^3
3	3	5	2	6		
6	7	7	6	6		
19	26	26	19	32	=	Sum of the columns
- 4	9	9	4	16	=	less the value of the diagonal of A squared (PCTs squared).
- 5	6	6	5	6	=	less the value of SCTs
10	11	11	10	10	=	TCTs

B) Freeman's Degree Measures

1. Absolute point degree centrality is defined as the number of adjacencies for a point in a graph. In other words, it is the total number of PCTs associated with a given corporation.
2. Relative point degree centrality is the proportion of points adjacent to the point of interest (sum of PCTs / n-1).

C) Freeman's Betweenness Measure

1. Absolute point betweenness centrality (g_{ij}) is the number of geodesics linking v_i and v_j. Let $g_{ij}(v_k)$ be the number of these geodesics containing v_k. Then the betweenness value of v_k with respect to the

point pair $v_i v_j$ is the ratio:

$$b_{ij}(v_k) = g_{ij}(v_k)/g_{ij} \tag{2}$$

where $b_{ij}(v_k)$ is the probability that point v_k falls on a randomly selected geodesic linking p_i and p_j. The overall centrality of a point is the sum of all betweenness values and is given as follows (Freeman, 1977, p.37):

$$c_B(v_k) = \sum_{j=1}^{n} \sum_{j=1}^{j-1} b_{ij}(v_k) \tag{3}$$

where n is equal to the number of points in the graph. $C_B(v_k)$ indexes the potential of a point for control by counting its opportunities for control. Freeman states it is the simplest and in many cases probably the most useful betweenness-based measure of centrality.

2. Relative point betweenness centrality is defined by the formula:

$$C'_B(v_k) = \frac{2c_B(v_k)}{n^2 - 3n + 2} \tag{4}$$

where $n^2 - 3n + 2$ is the maximum possible value of $C'_B(v_k)$.

D) Freeman's Closeness Measure

1. Absolute point closeness centrality, as stated in the text, is simply the sum of the geodesic distances for that particular point. Mathematically, closeness centrality of a point v_k is given as:

$$C_c(v_k) = \sum_{i=1}^{n} d(v_i, v_k) \tag{5}$$

where $d(v_i, v_k)$ is equal to the number of edges in the geodesic linking v_i and v_k.

2. Relative point closeness centrality is defined as:

$$c'_c(v_k) = \frac{(n-1)}{\sum_{i=1}^{n} d(v_i, v_k)} \quad (6)$$

Since $d(v_i, v_k)$ is equal to infinity for a unconnected point, $C_c(v_k)^{-1}$ is undefined for an unconnected graph.

E) Stephenson and Zelen Centrality Measure

Stephenson and Zelen's centrality is based on a statistical definition of 'information' where information is defined as the reciprocal of the variance of a single observation. Thus the information associated with a single path, s, is defined as

$$I_{ij}(S) = \frac{1}{D_{ij}(S)} \quad (7)$$

where D is the distance between point i and j.

Figure 3.8 is used to demonstrate the Stephenson-Zelen measure. The 'noise' of a transmission is measured by the variance of a signal going from X to Z, and is assumed to be 1. A path travelling from X-Y-Z involves two transmissions and, since variances are additive, the variance of the transmission is 2. Variance is also equal to distance if the variance is assumed equal to 1.

Consider the information that can be carried between points Y and Z in Figure 3.8. Y can send information through three independent paths, Y-Z, Y-X-Z, and Y-V-W-Z. The information of each path is, respectively, 1, 1/2 and 1/3. The combined path yields an information measure of 1.833 (1 + 1/2 + 1/3). In Figure 3.8, all paths between nodes are weighted the same. Stephenson and Zelen note that this procedure can also easily handle different weights for each path. For instance, this centrality measure could change the weights to reflect a quantitative matrix of the number of directors being delivered between corporations. In this respect, a matrix weighted by the number of directors shared between corporations would be analogous to the PDT, SDT and TDT measures developed by Hayden and Stephenson. Now consider the paths along which Y can send information to W. Y can send

Figure 3.8 Stephenson and Zelen's sample network

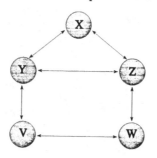

information to W through three non-independent paths: path 1 = Y-V-W, path 2 = Y-Z-W and path 3 = Y-X-Z-W. Obviously, path 2 and path 3 are not independent paths since they have the pair Z and W in common. Stephenson and Zelen's measure treats independent and non-independent paths differently. This centrality measure accounts for two paths that use a common pathway in the following manner. Consider the following definitions:

$D_{ij}(s)$ = number of lines in one path s.
$D_{ij}(r, s)$ = number of lines in common between paths r and s.

The matrix of these paths for Y and W is given as:

$$D_{YW} = \begin{bmatrix} 2 & 0 & 0 \\ 0 & 2 & 1 \\ 0 & 1 & 3 \end{bmatrix} \tag{8}$$

where the rows and columns correspond with paths 1, 2 and 3.

According to the above matrix, path 1 (Y-V-W) denotes the distance between Y and W as 2 and that path 1 does not share any common lines with paths 2 and 3. Path 2 (Y-Z-W) has two lines separating Y and Z and also shares one line (Z-W) with path 3. To find the combined path between Y and W and a calculation of information between these points, invert matrix D_{ij}. For the example D_{YW}, the inverse is:

$$D_{YW}^{-1} = 1/10 \begin{bmatrix} 5 & 0 & 0 \\ 0 & 6 & -2 \\ 0 & -2 & 4 \end{bmatrix} \tag{9}$$

The information in combined paths from Y to W is the sum of all the components of the D_{YW}^{-1} matrix (5/10 + 6/10 + 4/10 - 4/10) and is equal to 1.1 (11/10). The information in path Y and W is 10 percent more than if the points Y and W were incident (connected by a primary tie). This result highlights an important aspect of the Stephenson and Zelen measure. Although Y and Z do not share a common director, each is capable of transmitting more information through other multiple ties than through one PCT.

To determine the centrality of a point, first calculate the information of point i to all other points (I_{i1}, I_{i2} .... I_{in}). In the example above the information for point Y to points Z, W, V and X is 1.833, 1.1, 1.375 and 1.5714 respectively. As Zelen and Stephenson then state, 'the information on centrality of point i will be defined as the harmonic average of the information associated with the path from i to all other points' (p. 8). Mathematically, this is stated as:

$$I_1 = \frac{n}{\sum_{j=1}^{n} \frac{1}{I_{ij}}} \tag{10}$$

Thus the centrality measure for point Y is equal to 1.77 or 5/(1/1.833 + 1/1.1 + 1/1.375 + 1/1.5714).

F) Bonacich's Centrality Measure

Point centrality is defined by:

$$C_1 = r_{i1}c_1 + r_{i2}c_2 + ... + r_{in}c_n \tag{11}$$

where: n = number of corporations linked with i.
r_{ij} = intensity of a particular length.
C_j = centrality of organisations linked to i.

Let R be an N x N matrix of relationships, r_{ij}. Mariolis (1975) gives a definition of r as:

$$r_{ij} = \frac{b_{ij}}{\sqrt{d_i d_j}} \tag{12}$$

where: b_{ij} = number of members in common.

d_i and d_j = number of potential interlocks for each corporation.

R is a symmetric correlation type matrix.

In order to arrive at centrality measures, the C = RC system of equations needs to be solved simultaneously. C is a n x 1 vector of centrality scores and R is the n x n correlation matrix. As Bonacich (1972) points out, this system as it stands has no solution. In order to derive a solution, multiply C by the largest eigenvalue. Thus centrality scores are derived as follows:

$$C_i = (1/\lambda)\sum r_{ij} * C_j \tag{13}$$

λ is the eigenvalue of the first principal component. As Mizruchi states, 'this calculation is identical to factor analysis' (Mizruchi, 1982, p. 57). Mizruchi also demonstrates how the weighting system can be changed based on the corporate affiliation of each director. For instance, a CEO of corporation A sitting on corporation B's board is weighted more heavily than a simple interlocking directorship.

G) Freeman's Network Centrality Measure

In general, Freeman's three network centrality measures can be defined as:

$$C_x = \frac{\sum [C_x(v*) - C_x(v_i)]}{MAX \ \sum [C_x(v*) - C_x(v_i)]} \tag{14}$$

where: $C_x(v_i)$ = one of the three-point centralities defined above.

$C_x(v*)$ = largest value of $C_x(v_i)$ for any node in the network.

Max $\Sigma[C_x(v*) - C_x(v_i)]$ = maximum possible sum of differences in point centralities for a graph of n points.

NOTES

1. Terms to designate linkages, locks, deliveries and connectives should be prefixed with 'trans' rather than 'inter' in order to be consistent with transactional analysis. The prefix 'inter' is inconsistent with the understanding that relationships depend on transactional

beliefs, criteria, customs, policies, laws and rules that exist across and outside particular organisational transactions.

2. The sections on pp. 47-52 are taken from Hayden and Stephenson (1992).

3. A computer software program, *UCINET IV Version 1.0* (Borgatti, Everett and Freeman, 1992) directly calculates many of the techniques discussed in this paper. The program developed by Borgatti, Everett and Freeman contains a large assortment of the latest techniques used in network analysis.

4. Harary, Norman and Cartwright (1965) demonstrate various characteristics of a reachability matrix. Techniques are presented which can distinguish weakly connected blocks and strongly connected blocks in order to determine vulnerable points in the network.

5. A geodesic subgraph is an interesting result of a distance matrix. The geodesic subgraph shows all the corporations in which a message would have to pass in order to reach another corporation. To illustrate, assume corporation A can reach corporation B only through a TCT. The minimum distance in terms of a distance matrix would be a '3'. The geodesic subgraph would list all corporations that corporation A could go through in order to reach corporation B on a tertiary basis.

6. Although centrality implies power, controversy exists as to the validity of this association. Cook, Emerson, Gilmore and Yamagishi (1983) have shown that power does not necessarily equal centrality in exchange networks. Neale (1986) stated that just because central or core firms serve as a focal point, this does not necessarily mean they dominate other non-core firms. Others (Mizruchi, 1982; and Mintz and Schwartz, 1985) equate centrality with power. Social psychology literature experimentally shows that leadership roles typically devolve upon the individual in the most central position (Shaw, 1964). Bonacich (1987) has proposed different measures for both power and centrality.

7. For each of these three centrality measures, Freeman presents an absolute point measure and a relative point measure. The absolute measure is presented in the text, but the relative point measures are discussed in sections 1B, 1C and 1D in Appendix 3.2.

8. In effect this is a generalisation of the notion of a cut-point (Hage and Harary, 1983).

9. Through Bonacich's centrality measure, it is possible to account for the degree of overlap that is independent of group size. In other words, Bonacich argues that a corporation which has a large number of people sitting on a board of directors has more opportunity to share directors than a corporation with a smaller board. This increased opportunity to overlap should be taken into account. In this study, the emphasis on the size of the board of directors was not of interest, and therefore this aspect of Bonacich's measure was suppressed.

10. The Bonacich and Stephenson-Zelen measures are also able to incorporate the number of directorships within the analysis. Thus, each is able to provide quantitative as well as qualitative centrality measures.

REFERENCES

Bavelas, A. (1948), 'A Mathematical Model for Group Structure', *Human Organisation*, 7, 16-30.

Beije, P.R. and J. Groenewegen (1992), 'A Network Analysis of Markets', *Journal of Economic Issues*, 26, 87-114.

Bonacich, P. (1972), 'Technique for Analyzing Overlapping Memberships', *Sociological Methodology*, (ed.) by Herbert L. Costner. San Francisco: Jossey-Bass, Inc.

Bonacich, P. (1978), 'Using Boolean Algebra to Analyze Overlapping Memberships', *Sociological Methodology*, (ed.) by Karl F. Schuessler. San Francisco: Jossey-Bass, Inc.

Bonacich, P. (1987), 'Power and Centrality: A Family of Measures', *American Journal of Sociology*, 92, 1170-1182.

Borgatti, P., E. Everett and L. Freeman (1992), *UCINET IV Version 1.0*, Columbia: Analytic Technologies.

Burt, R.S. (1982), *Toward a Structural Theory of Action*. New York: Academic Press.

Caswell, J.A. (1987), 'Dominant Forms of Corporate Control in the U.S. Agricultural Sector', *American Journal of Agricultural Economics*, 69, 11-21.

Cook, K.S., R.M. Emerson, M.R. Gilmore and T. Yamagishi (1983), 'The Distribution of Power in Exchange Networks', *American Journal of Sociology*, 89, 275-305.

EPSCoR Project (1991), 'EPSCoR Planning Proposal'. Chancellor's Office. University of Nebraska. Lincoln, Nebraska (June).

EPSCoR Project (1992a), 'EPSCoR/NEB*SAT', Chancellor's Office. University of Nebraska. Lincoln, Nebraska (January).

EPSCoR Project (1992b), 'Nebraska NSF EPSCoR Implementation Project'. Chancellor's Office. University of Nebraska. Lincoln, Nebraska (February).

Freeman, L.C. (1977), 'A Set of Measure of Centrality Based on Betweenness', *Sociometry*, 40 (1), 35-41.

Freeman, L.C. (1979), 'Centrality in Social Networks: Conceptual Clarification', *Social Networks*, 1, 215-239.

Groenewegen, J. and P.R. Beije (1989), 'The French Telecommunication Industry Analyzed through the Network Approach: The Filière, and the Social Fabric Matrix', *Journal of Economic Issues*, 23, 1059-1074.

Hage, P. and F. Harary (1983), *Structural Models in Anthropology*. Cambridge: Cambridge University Press.

Harary, F., R.Z. Norman and D. Cartwright (1965), *Structural Models: An Introduction to the Theory of Directed Graphs*. New York: John Wiley and Sons, Inc.

Hayden, F.G. (1982), 'Social Fabric Matrix: From Perspective to Analytical Tool', *Journal of Economic Issues*, 16, 637-661.

Hayden, F.G. and K. Stephenson (1992), 'Overlap of Organizations: Corporate Transorganization and Veblen's Thesis on Higher Education', *Journal of Economic Issues*, 26, 53-85.

Hayden, F.G. and K. Stephenson (1993), 'Econometrics of Corporate Networks: A US Case Study'. *Research paper*, Group for Research and Advice in Strategic Management and Industrial Policy (GRASP), Erasmus University Rotterdam.

Leavitt, H.J. (1951), 'Some Effects of Communication Patterns on Group Performance', *Journal of Abnormal and Social Psychology*, 46, 38-50.

Liebhafsky, H.H. (1971), *American Government and Business*. New York: John Wiley and Sons, Inc.

Luce, R.D. and A.D. Perry (1949), 'A Method of Matrix Analysis of Group Structure', *Psychometrika*, 14, 95-116.

Mariolis, P. (1975), 'Interlocking Directorates and Control of Corporations: The Theory of Bank Control', *Social Science Quarterly*, 56, 425-439.

Means, G.C. (1939), *The Structure of the American Economy* (reprinted by Augustus M. Kelley: New York).

Meister, B.A. (1990), 'Analysis of Federal Farm Policy Using the Social Fabric Matrix', *Journal of Economic Issues,* 24, March, 189-224.

Mintz, B. and M. Schwartz (1985), *The Power Structure of American Business.* Chicago: University of Chicago Press.

Mizruchi, M. (1982), *The American Corporate Network.* Beverly Hills: Sage.

Munkirs, J. (1985), *The Transformation of American Capitalism: From Competitive Market Structures to Centralized Private Sector Planning.* New York: M.E. Sharpe.

Neale, W.C. (1986), 'The Transformation of American Capitalism. A Review Article', *Journal of Economic Issues,* 20, 203-209.

Pitofsky, R. (1978), 'The Political Content of Antitrust', Paper presented at University of Pennsylvania Conference on Antitrust Law and Economics, (November).

Sabidussi, G. (1966), 'The Centrality Index of a Graph', *Psychometrika,* 31, 581-603.

Shaw, M.E. (1964), 'Communication Networks', *Advances in Experimental Social Psychology,* vol. 1 (ed.) by L. Berkowitz. New York: Academic.

Sonquist, J.A. and T. Koenig (1975), 'Interlocking Directorates in the Top U.S. Corporations: A Graph Theory Approach', *Insurgent Sociologist,* 5, 196-229.

Stephenson, K. and M. Zelen (1989), 'Rethinking Centrality: Methods and Examples', *Social Networks,* 11, 1-37.

Stinchcombe, A.L. (1990), 'An Outsider's View of Network Analysis of Power' in: *Networks of Power: Organisational Actors at the National, Corporate, and Community Levels,* R. Perrucci and H.R. Potter (eds.). New York: Aldine de Gruyter.

US General Accounting Office (GAO) (1992), *University Research: Controlling Inappropriate Access to Federally Funded Research Results.* GAO/RCED 92-104. Washington DC: US General Accounting Office.

Warfield, J.N. (1976), *Societal Systems: Planning, Policy, and Complexity.* New York: John Wiley & Sons, Inc.

4. The Japanese Group

John Groenewegen

INTRODUCTION

In this chapter changes in Japanese business groups will be discussed. In the 1950s business groups like Sumitomo, Mitsubishi and Fuyo emerged out of clusterings around city banks. After examining the characteristics of such Japanese business groups, attention will be focused on three kinds of dynamics: first the changing role of the main bank and, related to that, the role of the market for corporate control, changes in the function of the General Trading Company and, finally, changes in subcontracting relations.

CHARACTERISTICS OF JAPANESE FIRMS AND GROUPS

Concepts

Traditionally firms are characterised as units where the power of decision making is in the hands of the manager (Alchian and Demsetz, 1972). In such classical firms the owner has the technological know-how, finances the investments, hires employees, fixes the wages and receives the 'residual' as profit. That type of firm has developed into new organisational structures via a growth in owners (the public corporation), via all kinds of financial relations (minority as well as majority participations) and via different contractual relations (supplier-buyer, transfer of technology and so on). Out of this growth in property and financial and contractual relations has arisen a firm which is often composed of several divisions, which has financial interests in other firms and which has relations of different kinds with other economic actors, including competitors, private and public research institutions, government agencies and the like. Because of the interrelations of an economic (supplier-buyer), financial (credit, cross shareholding), sociological (members of the same elite, *corps d'état*, or 'Old Boys' network) or personal (family relations, interlocking directorates) nature, a complex network comes into existence around the firm, which can be called a business group (Montmorillon, 1986, p. 57).[1] The firm can be considered the basic unit of decision making of the group in which resources are integrated, coordinated and controlled through an authority sytem (Whitley, 1990). The major strategic decisions are taken inside that basic unit. Such a firm can consist of several divisions operating in different markets. Such multi-divisional enterprises or strongly diversified firms are also often called 'groups'. We prefer to distinguish such multi-divisional diversified firms from the group and to reserve the latter for a cluster of autonomous firms which have a mutual interest and coordinate their activities to a certain degree. However, in concrete situations this distinction between a complex firm and a group is often not very clear because the coordination in a group can be realised through 'direction' or 'rule' (Goto, 1982). In the case of direction, the autonomous firms are so closely tied to the core firm that the group looks very much like a decision unit based on authority relations.

The Japanese Firm

The internal structure of the Japanese firm has been widely discussed, for instance by Aoki (1990). Productive organisation (the so-called J mode of production) in Japan is characterised by horizontal coordination resulting in an efficient use of onside information and effective adaptation to changing consumer demand and technologies. An internal labour market with job rotation makes the Japanese firm 'capability driven' instead of 'demand driven' (Imai and Itami, 1984). Supporting institutions include life-time employment, the seniority principle and company labour unions. These institutions certainly do not imply that employees enjoy a guaranteed career: life-time employment and the seniority principle apply to only 30 per cent of the workforce; moreover, the hierarchy of ranks is applied in such a way that promotion is based not only on years of service but on merit as well (Aoki, 1990).

Horizontal and Vertical Groups in Japan

Business groups can be found in every economy

> (...) but in Japan more than anywhere else, and unlike the situation in the United States, it is not the firm (corporation) but rather networks of firms (business groups) which are the key units organising the economy (Orrù, Hamilton and Suzuki, 1989, p. 550).

In the literature two kinds of groups are distinguished. Bieda (1970) makes a distinction between the loosely structured horizontal 'kinyo keiretsu' (type A in Goto, 1982 and the 'intermarket group' in Orrù, Hamilton and Suzuki, 1989) and the vertically structured 'sangyo keiretsu' (type B in Goto, 1982 and the 'independent group' in Orrù, Hamilton and Suzuki, 1989).

The horizontal business group is loosely structured and consists of a bank, a general trading company (GTC) and autonomous firms operating in almost all sectors of the economy ('one set for everything principle'; Bieda, 1970). Three of the post-war groups are considered to be successors of the pre-war 'zaibatsu' (literally 'financial clique'): Mitsui, Mitsubishi and Sumitomo.

However, the post-war groups differ fundamentally from the pre-war 'zaibatsu'. The old 'zaibatsu' were characterised by a holding company, strong family ties, feudal relations and specialisation in a few industries. In accordance with the Economic Deconcentration Law, the 'zaibatsu' were broken up after the war. However, around the city banks new groups emerged called 'kinyo keiretsu' (financially linked group; see Bieda, 1970). These groups have a rather loose structure. Members are linked together through different kinds of relations, of which the exchange of information in the so-called Presidents clubs is one of the most important. The presidents of the member firms regularly meet and exchange information about new technologies, new markets, government policies and the like (Goto, 1982). The firms are also linked through cross stockholding and interlocking directorates. Besides that, most loans are received from the group bank, whereas the GTC of the group plays a central role in suppling materials and the selling of products. The members of a 'kinyo keiretsu' often create joint subsidiaries for risky projects and often supply each other with intermediary goods. It is important to point out that relations are based on equality; none of the enterprises dominates the group. Group members are free to borrow from other banks and to use services of the GTC of another group. Besides the three successors of the 'zaibatsu', three other famous 'kinyo keiretsu' were formed after 1945: the Sanwa group and the Dai Ichi Kangin group (the so-called 'bank groups') and Fuyo (see Table 4.1).

Table 4.1 'Kinyo' and 'sangyo keiretsu' in Japan

Kinyo keiretsu	Sangyo keiretsu (top ten)
1. Mitshubishi	1. Tokai Bank
2. Mitsui	2. Industrial Bank of Japan
3. Sumitomo	3. Nippon Steel
4. Fuyo	4. Hitachi
5. Dai Ichi Kangin	5. Nissan
6. Sanwa	6. Toyota
	7. Matsushita
	8. Toshiba
	9. Tokyu
	10. Seibu

The second category of Japanese business groups (called 'sangyo keiretsu', type B or independent groups) are characterised by vertical relations between a dominating parent firm and several layers of subcontractors.

Instruments of Inter-firm Control in the 'Kinyo Keiretsu'

The horizontal relations of control in the 'kinyo keiretsu' are of an organisational, financial and economic nature.

At the organisational level three layers can be distinguished. Usually the highest organisational level of an intermarket group consists of the group bank, the GTC and the leading industrial firm. Beyond this nucleus the presidents of the leading firms in various sectors in which the group operates form the so-called Presidents Club. Below this presidental council, a larger committee coordinates the public relations of the group (Orrù, Hamilton and Suzuki, 1989). Another organisational relation comprises the large number of interlocking directorates among group members which contributes to networking and facilitates information exchange.

Financial relations concern reciprocal shareholding and loans. The firms do not hold many of each other's shares (between 2 and 7 per cent), but the combined holdings of group firms are between 20 and 30 per cent). Goto (1982) mentions shares of 0.7 per cent on average in the case of manufacturing firms, 2 per cent for trading companies and 5 per cent for banks. Orrù, Suzuki and Hamilton (1989) show that the insurance companies and banks hold relatively more shares of group members than do manufacturing firms. For instance, in the Mitsubishi group the top four stockholding firms are Meji Mutual Life Insurance, Mitsubishi Bank, Mitsubishi Trust and Banking, and Tokio M&F Insurance. Then follow Mitsubishi Heavy Industries and Mitsubishi Corporation. It can be concluded that the control of firms through shareholding is not so much a matter of individual firms but of the collectivity of firms. Also the relatively strong position of financial institutions should not be interpreted as control of the group by the banks. On the contrary, because firms hold shares of the banks, the financial institutions should be considered agents that operate on behalf of the group (Orrù, Hamilton and Suzuki, 1989).

Contrary to firms in Europe and the US, Japanese firms finance their investments largely by bank loans, in which of course the group bank plays an important role. The loan market is not a place of anonymous transactions between faceless suppliers and clients, but a market of 'implicit contracts' between actors with long-term business relations.

> (....) the loan market is not a place of 'anonymous' transactions where strangers happen to meet on business occasions but is a 'market of implicit contracts' in which banks, who are the lenders, and firms, who are the borrowers, enter into long term business relationships and the banks help the firms to stabilise their management (Tsutsui (1990, p. 53); quoted from Audretsch, 1989).

Aoki (1990) points out that banks are lenders as well as stockholders and in that position play an active role when firms perform badly. If firms do well, the group bank does not interfere in decisions, but when firms are in a difficult position the bank (in its role of lender of last resort) intervenes strongly in restructuring the firm, organising a financial rescue and replacing management.

Economic control relations concern horizontal buyer and supplier relations, the creation of joint subsidiaries (Goto, 1982) and the use group members make of services of the insurance company and the General Trading Company of the group. The GTC handles transactions of imports and exports as well as distribution in national markets. Roehl (1983) shows that the GTC is able to handle transactions at low cost when the products have the following characteristics: the product is standardised, the product is traded in large lots or very frequently, the product is handled by the GTC in several stages of the production chain and, finally, the product should have economies of scale in trading but also needs access to the world market for the realisation of these economies of scale. Roehl explains that the GTC is 'general' in the sense that it deals with a variety of products on the one hand and that it fulfils a variety of functions (warehousing, shipping, information, financing, services) on the other.

Horizontal control does not only exist within the 'kinyo keiretsu', but also between them. Each group owns stocks of firms belonging to other groups. Because that percentage is very limited, inter-group stockholding is often considered of little significance: the holdings are so small that the banks (which have most of the holdings in the other groups) cannot influence the economic policy of another group. Other researchers consider the inter-group holdings of strong symbolic value signaling 'reciprocal trust of all groups in each other's conduct of economic affairs' and showing that relations 'among groups is not one of all-out competition, but one of competition within the boundaries of a shared economic philosophy' (Orrù, Hamilton and Suzuki, 1989, p. 560).

Control in the 'Sangyo Keiretsu'

The 'sangyo keiretsu' are mainly very large industrial firms mostly operating in fast growing areas of the economy which demand heavy investments in R&D and large production plants. (Two of the independent groups shown in Tabel 4.1 are financial giants: Tokai Bank and the Industrial Bank of Japan.) The leading firm of the 'sangyo keiretsu' controls the subcontractors through the same relations as exist in the 'kinyo keiretsu': cross stockholding, interlocking directorates, supplier-buyer relations and loans. Goto (1982) explains that the instruments are alike, but that their intensity differs; for instance, the subcontractors in a 'sangyo keiretsu' depend completely on the demand of the parent firm, while management is supplied by the leading firm and not the other way around. In the 'sangyo keiretsu' vertical relations of dependency are dominant.

Relations between Inter-Market and Independent Groups

The six 'kinyo keiretsu' are the major shareholders of the leading firms in the independent groups, but none of the banks can control the leading firm. It can exercise power 'collectively, and in concert with the leading firm in the independent group' (Orrù, Hamilton and Suzuki, 1989, p. 562).

It is also important to take the financial power of the leading firm into account: for instance the Toyota group has so much financial strength that it is nicknamed 'Toyota Bank'. Orrù, Hamilton and Suzuki (1989) explain that the interrelation between the two types of groups has to do with their enormous investments which demand joint financing. A cooperative effort is often required to finance these investments, which 'prompts the creation of multiple partnerships'. Also the two financial groups, Tokai Bank and the Industrial Bank of Japan, have reciprocal shareholding with large industrial firms. The financial enterprises of the intermarket groups together with the independent bank groups form a 'horizontal web of financial enterprises, which share the financing of large industrial firms'.

> Therefore, if we take the independent groups together and consider all major shareholders in these groups we obtain a pattern similar to the one observed in each inter-market group. The independent groups form a 'maxi-inter-market group', where financial institutions are provided by inter-market and independent banks, and where the leading firms in the industrial groups are the members of the president's club. These patterns are similar to the ones found for the inter-market groups, but on a much larger scale (Orrù, Hamilton and Suzuki, 1989, p. 562).

DYNAMICS IN THE JAPANESE GROUPINGS

The picture presented above of Japanese groupings can be found in many studies. For the majority of the groups that picture still holds, but some important changes can be identified. In the following we first pay attention to the changing role of the Japanese government as an important environmental factor for business groups. Next we discuss changes in life-time employment and potential consequences for the 'J mode of production'. Finally, the changing role of the GTC and developments in the system of subcontracting are explored.

Role of the Japanese Government

The role of the Japanese government is legendary: the Ministry of International Trade and Industry (MITI) is the 'pilot organisation' of the developmental state (Johnson, 1982), a state that guides the structural development of the economy by means of industrial and technological policies. Important is the 'vision' by which long-term objectives with respect to sectoral developments are formulated. This vision is developed in consultation with business; in that process the bureaucrats of MITI play an important coordinating role. The basic idea behind this guiding role of the government is the failure of the market mechanism in providing sufficient information relevant for long-term investment decisions.

> To .... maintain and advance the private sector's vigorous development ... it is necessary to provide adequate information concerning the trends of domestic economy, international economy and industrial structure. It is particularly important to present a picture of the desired industrial structure, to achieve a national consensus on this, and to provide guidelines which facilitate the distribution of resources. These steps will spur creative

technological development and pioneering plant investment and will thus invigorate the market structure by encouraging effective competition (Industrial Structure Council, 1980; quoted from Aldershoff, 1982).

MITI has a longstanding tradition of effective intervention. In the fifties the 'production priority system' was applied to sectors like electric power, coal, iron and steel and chemical fertilisers. The development of these sectors was strictly regulated through control of the import of technology, control of credits, exemption from the Anti-Monopoly-Law and protection from foreign competitors. When Japan became a member of the OECD, IMF and GATT in the mid-sixties the government had to liberalise markets. Because business feared stiff competition in the mid-sixties the strong guidance of MITI was generally accepted. Legally based intervention was not allowed by the Keidanren, the 'keiretsu' and the Fair Trade Commission (see Johnson, 1982, on the so-called 'Special Measures Law'), but the development of a long-term 'vision' and 'administrative guidance' to realise the objectives of the 'visions' was generally accepted in Japanese society. That guidance is a mix of guidelines, warnings, recommendations and the like (Johnson, 1982), the effectiveness of which can only properly be understood in the context of Japanese decision making. Consultation between the vertical divisions of MITI ('genkyoku') and the branch associations, as well as the broader consultation in the Industrial Structure Council (ISC) together with the prestigious role of bureaucracy, give specific meaning to a 'warning' or a 'recommendation' of MITI.

In the first vision of 1963 the optimal industrial structure for the future was grounded on two criteria: income elasticity and productivity. Japan should concentrate industrial activities in sectors in which demand had a high income elasticity as well as sectors in which strong growth in productivity was to be expected. Heavy and chemical industries were presented as key sectors. Taking changing comparative advantages into account, the visions of the 1970s and 1980s stressed the importance of high tech knowledge-intensive sectors (computers, numerically controlled machine tools). Together with a change in focus in the visions, MITI changed its method of intervention from a rather direct one in the fifties into a more indirect approach from the mid-sixties onwards.

It would be a mistake to believe that all government intervention of MITI is effective. Kikkawa (1983) shows that industrial policy in stagnating sectors (shipbuilding) can be very effective, but that interventions in the expansion stage are of little use (automobile, computers). Technology policies in the introductory stage of a product's life cycle are considered of great importance, not because of subsidies, but more because of the organisational input of MITI in, for instance, research associations (Audretsch, 1989).

> With the institutional arrangement of research associations it became possible to undertake R&D projects jointly that were too common, too costly, too risky and/or too difficult for a single firm to tackle alone, thus solving the under-investment problem inherent in R&D investment (Goto and Wakasugi, quoted from Audretsch, 1989).

MITI often takes the initiative to organise a research association and negotiates with the Fair Trade Commission to exempt the association from the Anti-Monopoly Law.

A large part of R&D is financed by government; for example in 1985 half of the R&D programmes were subsidised, implying that the resulting innovations were also the property of the government. R&D can be organised in one of the 16 public laboratories under the direction of the Agency of Industrial Science and Technology (AIST) of MITI. MITI can also finance projects carried out in private research associations for 100 per cent. But in that case the patents also belong to MITI, which can distribute their information to any firm willing to pay a fee. R&D can also be financed with conditional loans, which firms have to repay when the R&D leads to profit-making activity within a seven-year period (for example, the project on large integrated circuits: VLSI).

Of course, the government also subsidises the R&D of private firms directly, but it is generally recognised that 'the Japanese government actually accounts for a smaller share of total R&D expenditures than do its Western counterparts' (Audretsch, 1989, p. 109).

The role of MITI has changed gradually towards indirect intervention and facilitating cooperation between firms in the introduction and stagnating stages of the product life cycle. Because of external developments (forced liberalisation of markets) and internal developments (growing financial and technological independence of firms), MITI lacked instruments for direct control over firms. Wisely MITI learned from the failures of its policies (automotive industry, consumer electronics, computers) and, after the beginning of the 1970s, focused its attention more and more on technology policy which implied a role as consultant and broker.

Changes inside the Firm

In 1992 and 1993 Japan had to confront its most severe crisis since 1945. To name a few examples: the consumer electronics industry is in trouble, Telecommunication (NTT) had to fire tens of thousands of people, the steel industry has to be restructured, Fujitsu (computers) is making its first losses since 1949 and Nissan is closing its factories in Zama. The system is seriously under pressure and firms are being forced to place large sections of their work force with affiliates or to 'suggest' early retirement. Life-time employment seems an illusion. Also the seniority principle is evaporating. As Aoki (1990) explained above, promotion and salary have been based partly on seniority and partly on merit. This seems to be changing and it is generally expected that rewards based on performance will play a larger role in the future.[2] Related to that the younger generation is willing to change positions between firms more often instead of accepting job rotation inside firms. If changes in life-time employment and the seniority principle become widespread then important pillars of the J-mode of production will be in danger. The more so because the role of banks as a guarantee for the survival of firms is also in question.

Changing Role of the Banks, a Market for Corporate Control?

The position of the main bank is changing because of the good financial reserves of many industrial firms. If the banks have ever been in a dominant position, this seems no longer to be the case. Competition among banks is increasing and will continue to increase due to the opening of the capital market which forces banks to become more efficient. Research indicates that Japanese banks are nowadays ranking clients according to their credibility and are also beginning to terminate relations with less attractive group members. Such an attitude was exceptional in the past, but has more and more become normal practice. On the other hand, firms no longer depend on banks as heavily as in the sixties and seventies. Of course, intense information exchange with the group bank still occurs and firms still lend money from them, but often this is considered more a matter of courtesy than a financial necessity (Kester, 1991). Also the practice of transferring retiring bank officers to management positions in related firms is waning. Although things are changing, banks and insurance companies still own a considerable (increasing) proportion of companies' outstanding shares (see Table 4.2). In the own industrial group the bank has a stable share ownership, although it is true that the banks do not use their legal 5 per cent and that the trend is downward (Table 4.3).

Table 4.2 Share-ownership by type of investors, all listed companies (per cent)

	'80	'81	'82	'83	'84	'85	'86	'87
Government and local government	0.2	0.2	0.2	0.2	0.2	0.2	0.8	0.9
Financial institutions	38.8	38.8	38.7	38.9	38.9	39.6	42.2	43.5
All banks	17.1	17.3	17.3	17.6	17.9	18.3	19.6	20.5
Investment trusts	1.9	1.5	1.3	1.2	1.0	1.1	1.3	1.8
Annuity trusts	0.5	0.4	0.4	0.4	0.4	0.5	0.7	0.9
Life insurance companies	12.3	12.5	12.6	12.6	12.7	12.7	13.5	13.3
Nonlife insurance companies	4.9	4.9	4.9	4.9	4.8	4.8	4.5	4.4
Other financial institutions	2.1	2.2	2.2	2.2	2.1	2.2	2.6	2.6
Business corporations	26.1	26.0	26.3	26.0	25.9	25.9	24.1	24.5
Securities companies	2.0	1.7	1.7	1.8	1.9	1.9	2.0	2.5
Individuals & others	30.4	29.2	28.4	28.0	26.8	26.3	25.2	23.9
Foreigners	2.5	4.1	4.7	5.1	6.3	6.1	5.7	4.7
TOTAL	100.0	100.0	100.0	100.0	100.0	100.0	100.0	100.0

Source: Kester, 1991, p. 199.

Table 4.3 Major bank equity holdings in its industrial group

	1975	1980	1985	1986
The Fuji Bank, Ltd.	4.7	4.4	3.9	3.8
The Sumitomo Bank, Ltd.	4.9	3.9	3.6	3.5
The Mitsubishi Bank, Ltd.	4.9	4.0	4.0	3.9
The Sanwa Bank, Ltd.	4.1	4.1	3.8	3.7
The Dai-Ichi Kangyo Bank, Ltd.	4.3	4.3	4.0	3.8
The Mitsui Bank, Ltd.	3.3	3.5	3.7	3.6
AVERAGE	4.4	4.0	3.8	3.7

Source: Kester, 1991, p. 209.

Market for Corporate Control

The Anglo-American market for corporate control is characterised by many unfriendly takeovers. Firms can buy shares from a diffused ownership, concentrate them in the hands of a few who can then replace management and change strategy. Mergers or takeovers of a conglomerate type are often undertaken because management wants to diversify, to replace the management of competitors or to restructure activities between firms. Cross subsidisation or efficient allocation of capital are also well-known arguments for a conglomerate type of diversification in Anglo-American economies. In Japan the need for takeovers for these reasons is felt less because management can realise these objectives through group membership (Imai and Itami, 1984); in fact, management prefers to achieve the objectives of horizontal mergers (reduction of overcapacity, restructuring of sectors) in cartels under the umbrella of MITI. Due to these differences the market for corporate control in Japan is completely different from the Anglo-American one. Takeovers are rare in Japan and unfriendly takeovers still very exceptional. This is due not to legal or regulatory restrictions (Kester, 1991), but to barriers of another kind. The existence of industrial groupings with exclusive cross shareholding is an important barrier. Also implicit contracts with different stakeholders would incur enormous costs in situations of recontracting. Last but not least there is a cultural barrier: selling a firm is like selling a family. Although public opinion is changing in this respect (bureaucrats of MITI and especially the Keidanren are increasingly in favour of a more liberalised market for corporate control), the general attitude of management is certainly not in favour of unfriendly takeovers.

So far takeovers in Japan are of a friendly nature, focusing on growth of market share. Big deals are all within the province of MITI and supported by the main bank, whereas the smaller ones take place within the framework of the industrial groups. Takeovers of small firms are generally of a friendly nature involving parties which have a longstanding relationship.

For foreign companies it is extremely difficult and costly to takeover a Japanese firm. The ones available are small family-owned firms having no ties with main Japanese banks, suppliers or customers. The attractive firms are mostly members of complicated networks which are very difficult for foreign firms to penetrate. Recently the case of T. Boone Pickens and Koito clearly showed how closed the Japanese system is. T. Boone Pickens had purchased a 20 per cent share in Koito, a halogen lights producer and main supplier of Toyota (which also had a 20 per cent share). Kester (1991) believes that the succesful attempts of Toyota to get T. Boone Pickens out of Koito were not based on fear of losing control to a foreigner, but on the wish to keep information about internal transfer prices among group members and away from foreign companies. (Such information could be important in proving Japanese firms were quilty of pedatory pricing.)

It can be concluded that the position of main banks in the business groups is changing towards less strong links. At the same time a market for corporate control is emerging, but of a completely different type then the one known in the US and the UK. It is expected that in Japan takeovers will remain mainly of a friendly nature and the result of long-standing relationships.

The General Trading Company

Traditionally the General Trading Company (GTC) fulfils several functions for group members, but also for outsiders. The GTC realises economies of scale and scope in producing information and organising trade. Because information is produced with high fixed costs, it is efficient for different firms to use the same information about specific regions, consumer preferences or trade regulations. Yanamura (1976) points out that the GTC also reduces risks with respect to fluctuations in foreign currencies (the GTC imports and exports from the same country) and with respect to variations in demand (a decline in one market can be compensated for by growth in another). The GTC offers all kinds of services related to import and export, provides turn-key projects and is involved in so-called third country trade (a Japanese GTC takes care of the trading between two countries other than Japan).

In order to understand why Japanese trading companies are 'general', researchers often make use of transaction costs analysis (Roehl, 1983; Shin, 1989). Suppose a trading company takes care of the export of a manufactured product with very specific characteristics. Suppose further that the GTC has undertaken specific investments in order to produce information about consumers and has also made the product known to the public by means of an intensive advertising campaign. Then all conditions for opportunistic behaviour by the manufacturer are fulfilled: he can bypass the trading company and make opportunistic use of the prior investments of the GTC. Shin (1989) explains that the GTC has possibilities to 'safeguard' its investments but, because of rising transaction costs, it can never safeguard itself completely in cases of asset specificity. GTCs are thus efficient in cases where transaction specific investments are negligible and possibilities for opportunism are small. When investments become specific to particular needs of the contracting parties, opportunism is possible and internalisation of trading into the firm becomes more efficient. This will be the case with highly differentiated consumer durables and special industrial machinery. Facts about the role of the Japanese GTC are in line with this hypothesis of transaction cost theory. Trading companies have a relatively large share of trading in commodities like food and tobacco, textiles and wood, pulp and paper. Their role is much smaller in the category of machinery and equipment. The analysis of Shin (1989) also shows that the role of the GTC is smaller in exports than in imports, which is understandable because Japanese exports are more sophisticated than imports. The 'generality' of the trading company is also reflected in its larger role in new and small markets compared to established differentiated ones, as well as a relatively larger role in regions like Southeast Asia, Africa, the Middle East and Latin America compared to its role in the US and Europe.

As exports become more and more specific, with manufacturers creating their own distribution channels and bypassing the General Trading Companies, and as Japanese firms increase their direct foreign investments, the role of the GTC will decrease further. In response to these negative developments, it is to be expected and can already be observed that the GTC will become less 'general' and will focus more on specific regions and sectors.

Subcontracting

The subcontracting system described above as the 'sangyo keiretsu' is the classic model of the pyramid, with advantages for the parent firm based on specialisation, 'just-in-time' delivery and quality control. For the supplier the advantage is to be found in long-term stable relations in which financial, technological and managerial assistance are important. The classic model of subcontracting is a situation of dependency of the supplier, who is locked into a relationship with a large customer.

In the system of supplying large firms, developments are taking place which are characterised as INTAC (Inter-industrial Network for Technological Activities, see Furukawa, Teramoto and Kanda, 1990), or 'Igyoushu Kouryu' (Van Kooij, 1991). According to these developments the pyramid is replaced by a cobweb in which cooperating Small and Medium Sized Enterprises (SMEs) play a more powerful role in relating to the large customer. In general, networks can be described as governance structures in which autonomous firms interact and have common interests. Their activities are more or less coordinated, depending on the tightness of the network. Networks can be very close with one central spider, or can be of a looser nature with equal actors. Networks can be explained on efficiency grounds in respect to economies of scope: diversification inside the hierarchy is one way to realise economies of scope, and networking is another. In networks information about highly differentiated consumer demand or technologies can be efficiently transferred from one sector to another. For the individual firm, that means fewer sunk costs, implying less vulnerability to opportunism.

In Japan the INTAC have shown most growth since 1985 when MITI started to stimulate those kinds of networks (Furukawa, Teramoto and Kanda, 1990). The appreciation of the yen, increased competition from the Newly Industrialised Economies (NIEs), the globalisation of Japanese industry, the acceleration of technological development and highly differentiated consumer demand are all factors which, in addition to the stimulating measures of MITI, are contributing to the emergence of networks of SMEs (Van Kooij, 1991).

CONCLUSION

As with all economic systems, the Japanese one is constantly changing. Pressures from outside as well as from inside are causing the Japanese business system to adapt. It is difficult the assess the nature and extent of the changes we have discussed in this chapter. Are we observing the beginning of a fundamental change in the system, or are the developments discussed just adaptations of the system? Such questions have also been raised in the past, but could never be satisfactorily answered because of the complex of interdependent elements involved. Two of these are worth mentioning here: economic efficiency and the wider cultural context.

Among others Aoki (1990) explains that the 'J-mode of production' is efficient in situations of incremental changes in the environment, whereas radical changes in technology, for instance, cannot be handled efficiently in the 'J mode'. Therefore, one could presumably expect to find the 'J-mode of production' in specific sectors in different economies. Suppose incremental change is a characteristic of the automotive industry: one would then expect to find the 'J-mode' in that sector in all economies. Such an efficiency approach assumes that managements of firms change their models of production according to general efficiency standards and that a selection mechanism exists that makes the 'fittest survive'. However, models of production do not differ so much between sectors, but more between economic systems; this gives rise to the idea that there is more involved than economic efficiency, for example differences in the wider cultural context. Imai and Itami (1984) point to the wider context of the 'social fabric' as an explanatory variable for differences in the organisation of production and the role and dynamics of firms. Orrù, Hamilton and Suzuki argue in the same vein and conclude that in terms of Japanese groups:

> the patterns of vertical and horizontal control can only be understood meaningfully in their institutional context; these patterns embody cultural and normative prescriptions which inform the organisational strategies that have led to Japan's economic success (Orrù, Hamilton and Suzuki, 1989, p. 569).

Strategic management is also developed in the cultural, social and political context in which markets and firms are embedded. Moreover, firms develop their own corporate culture and identity which result in routines of decision making and tacitness of knowledge (Dietrich, 1991). Pressure on management from outside or internal developments, then, do not necessarily result in the same adaptations and changes in the structure of firms and groups. On the contrary: general changes in the environment are 'filtered' in business systems and firms where the cultural context plays a crucial role.

Changes in Japanese business groups result from external and internal pressures and from strategic management, all embedded in a wider cultural environment. A complex of interdependent variables is involved which makes it difficult to say whether the changes we observe are 'superficial' or more fundamental. Clearly important changes are taking place in Japan and that in itself is reason enough to monitor these developments closely.

NOTES

1. 'Quels qu'ils soient, ces éléments sont en liaison les uns avec les autres: liaison patrimoniale, liaison financière ou liaison contractuelle. Et ces relations sont dotées de stabilité (ce qui ne veut pas dire qu'elles soient rigides ou définitives). L'agencement de ces interrelations - ou organisations - produit une unité complexe (ou système ou groupe) qui se dégage en tant que telle' (Montmorillon, 1986, p. 57).
2. Survey among managers published in NRC Handelsblad of 18 March, 1993.

REFERENCES

Aldershoff, W.G. (1982), 'Anticiperend economisch-structuurbeleid in Japan', *ESB*, 28 July, 768-771.

Alchian, A.A. and H. Demsetz (1972), 'Production, Information Costs, and Economic Organisation', *American Economic Review*, 777-795.

Aoki, M. (1990), 'Toward an Economic Model of the Japanese Firm', *Journal of Economic Literature*, XXVIII, March, 1-27.

Audretsch, D.B. (1989), 'Joint R&D and Industrial Policy in Japan', in A.N. Link and G. Tassey (eds.), *Cooperative Research and Development*. Dordrecht/Boston: Kluwer Academic Publishers.

Bieda, K. (1970), *The Structure and Operation of the Japanese Economy*, Sydney: John Wiley.

Dietrich, M. (1991), 'European Economic Integration and Industrial Policy', *Review of Political Economy*, 3 (4), 418-438.

Fruin, W.M. (1992), *The Japanese Enterprise System*. Oxford: Clarendon Press.

Furukawa, K., Y. Teramoto and M. Kanda (1990), 'Network Organisation for Inter-firm R&D Activities: Experience of Japanese Small Business', *Technology Management*, 5, (1), 27-41.

Goto, A. (1982), 'Business Groups in a Market Economy', *European Economic Review*, 19, 53-70.

Goto, A. and R. Wakasugi (1987), 'Technology Policy in Japan: A Short Review', *Technovation*, 5, 269-279.

Groenewegen, J. (1990), *Business Groups in Japan and South Korea*, paper presented at the EARIE conference in Lisboa, September, Rotterdam: Erasmus University.

Imai, K. and H. Itami (1984), 'Interpenetration of Organisation and Market', *International Journal of Industrial Organisation*, 2, 285-310.

Industrial Structure Council (1980), *Industrial Structure Policy for the 1980s (excerpt)*, March.

Johnson, Ch. (1982), *MITI and The Japanese Miracle*. Stanford, California: Stanford University Press.

Kester, W.C. (1991), *Japanese Take-overs*. Boston MA: Harvard Business School Press.

Kikkawa, M. (1983), '*Shipbuilding, Motorcars and Semiconductors, the Diminishing Role of Industrial Policy in Japan*', in: G. Shepherd, F. Duchène and Ch. Sanders (eds.), Europe's Industries; Public and Private Strategies for Change. London: Pinter.

Koshiro, K. (1986), 'Japan's Industrial Policy for New Technologies', *Journal of Institutional and Theoretical Economics*, 142, 163-177.

Montmorillon, B. de (1986), *Les Groupes Industriels*. Paris: Economica.

Okumura, H. (1982), 'Inter-firm Relations in an Enterprise Group', *Japanese Economic Studies*, 10, 53-82.

Orrù, M., G.G. Hamilton and M. Suzuki (1989), 'Patterns of Inter-firm Control in Japanese Business', *Organisational Studies*, 10 (4), 549-574.

Roehl, T. (1983), 'A Transaction Cost Approach to International Trading Structure: The Case of the Japanese General Trading Companies', *Hititsubashi Journal of Economics*, 24, 119-135.

Shin, K. (1989), 'Information, Transaction Costs, and the Organisation of Distribution: the Case of Japan's General Trading Companies', *Journal of the Japanese and International Economies*, 3, 292-307.

Tsutsui, Y. (1990), 'Japan's Banking Industry: Collusion under Regulation', *Japan Economic Studies*, 53-92.

Van Kooij, E. (1991), 'Japanese Subcontracting at a Crossroads', *Small Business Economics*, 3, 145-154.

Whitley, R.D. (1990), 'East Asian Enterprise Structures and the Comparative Analysis of Forms of Business Organisation', *Organisation Studies*, 11, (1), 47-74.

Yanamura, K. (1976), 'General Trading Companies in Japan - Their Origins and Growth', in H. Patrick (ed.), *Japanese Industrialization and Its Social Consequences*. Berkely: University of California Press.

5. Dynamics of Enterprises; (R)evolution of a Large Enterprise: A Case Study of Philips Electronics N.V.

Paul Merkelbach[*]

INTRODUCTION

> Cycle racing events like the Tour de France are intelligent combinations of individual ability, technology, structural and ad hoc cooperation and environmental circumstances. Worldwide competition in the electronics industry is not so very much different. However a complicating factor is that some participants ignore the rules of the game: the most open and liberal society is always at a disadvantage (Prestowitz, 1988).

In this chapter the case of Philips Electronics NV will be studied, not in terms of mere description of the company's history and development, but the evolution of this enterprise within the context of relevant environmental trends. Starting points will be the fact that Keynesian macroeconomics is inappropriate in an open economy and that the emphasis on the market as the sole mechanism for stimulating efficiency and dynamics is contradicted by the growing importance of a new mix of competition and cooperation (Mytelka, 1991).

In the first section some major quantitative indicators in the total electronics industry will be presented: these include evolution of production in the electronics sector worldwide and of production in the different subsectors, including a forecast for the near future; comparison between

[*]The author of this paper works for Philips Electronics. Many of the facts and figures that could be used are company-confidential; those presented here are all available from public sources. It should also be stated that whatever views are expressed in this paper, they pertain to the author himself and should in no way be considered the views of Philips Electronics.

market and production per region and per subsector; and major competitors in the subsectors in which these companies are active.

The second section will show a much more qualitative outline of the key environmental trends which the electronics industry has to face. These will be presented under the headings: economic/political, market, industry and technology.

The second section will also focus on the importance of electronics for present and future society. This is the key to the interactive relation between governments and the industry, which in turn constitutes a major and often determining environmental factor for it.

The third section will present the case of Philips Electronics against the background of quantitative and environmental trends. Apart from a short history of the company, this part will deal with its strengths and weaknesses, with the so-called centurion process and with the answers of Philips to the changing environment.

In the fourth section some thoughts will be presented on the future of the electronics industry in the world, of the electronics industry in Europe, and of the environment necessary for a company like Philips Electronics to continue playing a key role.

MAJOR QUANTITATIVE INDICATORS

The electronics industry is not always defined in the same way. To provide a consistent view, use has been made of one single source to collect the quantitative trends presented here: EIC (Electronics International Corporation).

The evolution of markets in the electronics sector worldwide is indicated in Table 5.1.

One yardstick to judge the strengths and weaknesses of companies is the competitive situation in what these companies consider to be their home market. By comparing the markets and production in different parts of the world, this home market competition can be indicated. Table 5.2 shows the market and production of the electronics industry per geographical region in 1990.

Evident strong European production (25 per cent larger than the market and regional production greater than 25 per cent of world production) does not exist in any subsector. Evident weak European production (25 per cent smaller than the market and regional production smaller than 25 per cent of world production) does exist in consumer products, active components and office automation. A subsector in which European companies play in the

Dynamics of the firm

Table 5.1 Markets in the electronics sector ($ billion)

Product categories[1]	1984[2]	1990	1996 (projec- tion)[3]	average growth rate 1990/1996
Data Processing	105	227	374	9%
Software and Services	42	145	326	14%
Professional Electronics Equipment	54	101	147	6%
Consumer Products	50	88	110	4%
Active Components	38	75	140	11%
Telecommunications	38	67	91	5%
Passive Components	31	57	84	7%
Measurement/Instrumentation	29	49	70	6%
Automation/Industrial Data Processing	25	53	92	10%
Office Automation	22	27	33	3%
Medical Electronics	9	19	27	6%
Total	443	908	1494	7%

1. See Appendix 5.1 for the product categories.
2. The figures for 1984 are not really comparable with those for 1990. Volatile currency exchange rates had a major impact (for example, in 1989 the Yen/Guilder ratio increased by 40 per cent) and not every subsector was of the same importance in the major currency regions. Nevertheless, the evolution of the markets given in Table 5.1 can at least be seen as a trend.
3. To estimate the figures for the trend to 1996, any breaking of political or economic ties (embargo, partial or total border closing, massive relocation of production) or major differentials of inflation and exchange rates are excluded. It is however estimated that the US $ is significantly undervalued and will reach the ECU-value, that the Yen is overvalued and that the inflation rate will be at 3 per cent per annum.

world league, consumer products, seems weak instead of strong. Evident strong US production does not exist either in any subsector. Evident weak US production exists in consumer products. Evident strong Japanese production exists in several subsectors: consumer products, active components and office automation. Evident weak Japanese production does not exist in any subsector. As to the rest of the world, emerging strength can be seen in data processing and in consumer products. Measured by this yardstick, European electronics production has more weaknesses than strengths. The opposite is true for Japanese production.

Many other methods exist to judge the competitive strength of a company, like R&D expenditure, patents and so on. Because the main purpose of this section is simply to present a quantitative environment for Philips Electronics, such that the competitive position of this company can be judged in an indicative way, more quantitative data is not considered of value. Less quantitative, but very important as to the total environment of a company, is information on the major competitors and the subsectors in

Table 5.2 Market and production of the electronics industry per region in 1990 ($ billion)

	Market				Production			
	1	2	3	4	1	2	3	4
Data Processing	77	84	39	27	57	84	53	33
Software and Services	40	69	19	17	38	75	17	15
Prof. Electronics Equip.	28	48	7	18	31	53	8	9
Consumer Products	28	23	16	21	16	11	36	25
Active Components	15	22	27	11	11	20	36	8
Telecommunications	23	19	11	14	24	17	14	12
Passive Components	16	18	15	8	14	17	19	7
Measurement/Instrum.	16	17	7	9	17	20	9	3
Automation/Industrial								
Data Processing	15	17	14	7	13	19	17	4
Office Automation	7	11	4	5	5	9	10	3
Medical Electronics	5	7	3	4	6	8	4	1
Total	270	335	162	141	232	333	223	120

1 = Europe 2 = US 3 = Japan 4 = Rest of the world (ROW)

which they are active. Table 5.3 provides for information on major competitors (holding a market share greater than 5 per cent) per electronics subsector and per geographical sector.

Table 5.3 Major competitors per electronics subsector and region (1990)

Europe	US	Japan	World
Data Processing			
IBM	IBM	Fujitsu	IBM
BULL	DEC	Hitachi	DEC
DEC	Unisys	IBM	Fujitsu
Fujitsu		NEC	NEC
Olivetti		Unisys	
Siemens		Toshiba	
Software and Services			
Cap Gemini Sogeti	GM/EDS	NTT	GM/EDS
Finsiel	ADP	CSK	
	CSC	NBC	
	EDS	NCC	
	TRW		

Europe	US	Japan	World
Professional			
Electronic equipment	General Motors	Mitsubishi	General motors
GEC	General Electric	NEC	
Thomson	Raytheon	Fujitsu	
		Sony	
		Toshiba	
Consumer Products			
Philips	Matsushita	Matsushita	Matsushita
Thomson	Thomson	Sony	Sony
Bosch	Philips	Hitachi	Hitachi
Grundig	Sony	Pioneer	Philips
Hitachi	Toshiba	Sanyo	Sanyo
Matsushita	Zenith	Sharp	Thomson
Nokia		Toshiba	Toshiba
Sony			
Active Components			
Philips	Intel	Hitachi	Hitachi
Thomson	Motorola	NEC	Motorola
Motorola	Texas	Toshiba	NEC
Siemens	Toshiba	Fujitsu	Toshiba
		Matsushita	
		Mitsubishi	
Measurement/			
Instrumentation			
HP	HP	HP	HP
Siemens		Hitachi	
		Matsushita	
		NEC	
Telecommunication			
Alcatel Altsthom	ATT	Fujitsu	ATT
Siemens	Northern Telecom	Matsushita	Alcatel Alsthom
Ericsson	Siemens	NEC	NEC
GEC		Hitachi	Northern
		OKI	Telecom
			Siemens
Passive Components			
Nihil	Nihil	Nihil	Nihil
Automation/Industrial			
Data Processing			
IBM	DEC	Nihil	IBM
Siemens	IBM		

Europe	US	Japan	World
Office Automation			
Cannon	Cannon	Cannon	Canon
Ricoh	Xerox	Fuji-Xerox	Ricoh
Xerox	Kodak	Minolta	Xerox
Minolta	Minolta	Ricoh	Minolta
Mita	Ricoh	Konica	
OCE		Mita	
		Sharp	
Medical Electronics			
GE	GE	Hitachi	GE
Philips	Siemens	Toshiba	Philips
Siemens	Picker	Fukuda	Siemens
	Medtronic	GE	Toshiba
	Philips	Shimadzu	

MAJOR QUALITATIVE TRENDS

The electronics industry faces many key qualitative environmental trends. Some of these trends are relevant for other industrial or service sectors as well. However, the electronics industry is one of the very few sectors where the main players have transformed themselves from local companies, via international companies, via global companies to multinational and sometimes to transnational companies. This transformation process has resulted in an environment that is rather specific to this one sector. This specific position is reinforced by the growing recognition of the importance of electronics for present and future society and the interactive relation between governments and industry in terms of this recognition.

Key Environmental Trends

The key environmental trends especially relevant for the electronics industry concern the economic/political environment, the market, the industry and technology.

Economic/political
- volatile currency exchange rates between geographical blocs (for example in 1989 the Yen/Guilder ratio increased by 40 per cent), with significant consequences for a flexible balance of sourcing and selling and with a strong impact on competitive positions;

- multiple political forces and changing alliances (US, Europe, Japan, Eastern Europe, China), with consequences for political risk analysis and flexible investments;
- recognition of the importance of electronics for present and future society. This recognition is not new as is reflected, for instance, in the control lists used by the Coordinating Committee for Multilateral Export Control (COCOM) containing the most strategic products to be exported only with explicit government permission. These lists primarily comprise electronic products and technology. At present this recognition is also translated into an interactive relationship between industry and governments, resulting in so-called push and pull projects.

Market

- demand across the industrialised world will become more uniform, but at the same time the market will ask for more diversification in products and services;
- markets increasingly demand 'system' solutions rather than isolated products and services, requiring important changes in the way (some) companies operate;
- professional markets and consumer markets are no longer separated, with consequences for integrated product and market approaches;
- the share of software and services in electronics is growing very fast.

Industry

- the number of global competitors is growing, so are their specialisation and cooperation ventures;
- investments in R&D expenditure and fixed assets needed to remain a key player are escalating. This process is reinforced by shorter life cycles of products. This trend demands selectivity (few companies are likely to build world leadership in more than 5 or 6 fundamental competences) (Hamel and Prahalad, 1990) and risk sharing through strategic alliances and collaborative ventures. At the same time, innovation becomes a key competitive weapon. Innovation must therefore be managed professionally and not left to chance;
- increasing importance of downstream activities (that is sales, service and logistics) *vis à vis* manufacturing with consequences for the total value-added chain and at the same time concentration and globalisation of distribution channels, with important consequences for existing balances of power (Porter, 1980 and 1985).

Technology

. rapid advance of optical technology;
. race towards submicron VLSI technology, with complex projects belonging to this development;
. the speed of IC design becomes crucial in the context of fast market response. This requires reassessment of investments in IC manufacturing versus IC design;
. computer integrated manufacturing (CIM) will make the costs of manufacturing less location-dependent, opening opportunities to spread industrial activity more widely;
. breakthroughs in software productivity;
. integration of information technology, communication technology and entertainment functions, with major challenges for consumer interfaces (*Wall Street Journal*, 1992).

This listing of key environmental trends is far from exhaustive. Its only purpose is to indicate the complexity of the world the electronics industry has to operate in and to suggest the direction developments will most probably take. This direction can be summarized in terms of four main elements: globalisation, concentration/cooperation, technological progress and the importance of software.

Importance of Electronics

The environment of the electronics industry is increasingly determined by the growing recognition of the importance of this sector for present and future society. The development of society is heavily influenced by waves of technology. In the industrial area, the first important wave lasted from 1790 to 1840 and was based largely on textile industry technologies harnessing coal and steam power. The second wave took place from 1840 to 1890 and drew directly on the development of railways and the mechanisation of production. The third wave ran from 1890 to 1940 and was based on electric power, advances in chemistry and the internal combustion engine. The current wave is based on electronics and seems to be running longer, faster and with greater impact than all the previous waves combined.

The world electronics industry is already extensive and has the potential to become the largest manufacturing industry within the next 10 years. By the year 2000, the electronics industry could have outgrown all other manufacturing industries; a substantial part of all manufactured products will consist of electronics and about 80 per cent of all economic activity will be heavily dependent on electronics.

This process is already well under way. In Germany, for example, 10 per cent of all those employed work in electronics and 72 per cent in sectors such as machinery, automotives and chemicals which rely on electronics (Philips International, 1989; Commission of the European Communities, 1991).

Governments tend to accept more and more that electronics will be the largest and most important manufacturing industry within a short time and will provide the foundation on which the economies of advanced countries are based. Moreover, it is generally recognised that electronics provides the building blocs of infrastructures for communication, information, administration, education and defence. This acceptance is the key to a growing interactive relation between governments and the electronics industry, a relation that in itself is a major environmental factor for electronics.

For the electronics industry, then, the Porter line of thinking is more than just theory: Government is not so much an independent factor, but an actor which influences the way the diamond of the nation functions. So all kinds of public policies in the field of education, R&D, taxation, anti-trust measures, standardisation, consumer protection, infrastructure, information, government procurement, etc., must as much as possible enhance competition, innovation, upgraded quality strategies and long-term commitment (Porter, 1990).

PHILIPS ELECTRONICS

From Local to Transnational

Philips Electronics, its history and its present situation can be understood only against the background of its transition from a local to a transnational enterprise.

The local enterprise produces and sells in one and the same country. After its foundation in 1891 Philips was active as a local enterprise for only a few years.

The international enterprise produces in its home land. However, sales, inclusive dealer networks and service facilities however take place in foreign markets as well. Car manufacturers for a long time were model international enterprises. Philips was such an enterprise around the turn of the century. The organisational structure of an international enterprise is very centralised, with foreign branches having only executive power.

The global enterprise not only sells abroad, but also produces in other countries. These foreign productions are limited, however, to the minimum necessary to counterbalance environmental influences like import restrictions or prohibitive transport costs. The foreign production of these enterprises is often limited to some form of assembly operation. To some degree, all companies operating in international markets sometimes function on this level. Some companies however are still characterised by this phase in the transition process, for example a number of large Japanese enterprises.

The multinational enterprise not only sells abroad, but has fully integrated production facilities in many countries. The most common company strategy in this case can be described as 'local-for-local'. Within the multinational company the national organisations have considerable power as they are integrated in the structure and the economy of the host countries. Because of the protectionist environment caused by the economic crisis of the thirties, Philips at that time developed into a multinational company with strong national organisations and national production centres: local factories making local products for local markets under local management control. The corporate structure consisted of the corporate headquarters and the headquarters of the product divisions and of a central research and development organisation. This situation existed until the eighties.

The transnational enterprise is characterised by a network organisation. For many products, local-for-local production has been replaced by centralised production for the world market. This change is most common in production in which economies of scale are important, transportation costs are limited and standardisation is worldwide. The transnational enterprise focuses on worldwide products, production and marketing concepts. The prime role of the national organisations as existed within the multinational enterprise disappears. Many multinational companies are now transforming into transnational companies, among them Philips; many national production centres (NPC) are being closed down or restructured as international production centres (IPC) take their place; the matrix structure of national organisations and product divisions changes and IPC come under international product division management control.

Philips Electronics, started in 1891 as a local lamp factory, is now developing into a transnational, diversified, industrial and software electronics company with:

. nine product divisions;
. 272 factories in 47 countries (141 in Europe, 54 in North America, 36 in Asia and 41 in the rest of the world);
. 60 national sales organisations;
. marketing and sales outlets in 150 countries;

- a strong technology base with R&D taking up to 7 per cent of sales; research laboratories in five countries; 60,000 patents and 10,000 inventions;
- a multinational workforce of 240,000 (55 per cent in Europe, 16 per cent in North America, 14 per cent in Asia and 15 per cent in the rest of the world);
- assets amounting to Fl. 50 billion (66 per cent in Europe, 17 per cent in North America, 11 per cent in Asia and 6 per cent in the rest of the world);
- a turnover of Fl. 57 billion (58 per cent in Europe, 23 per cent in North America, 10 per cent in Asia and 9 per cent in the rest of the world), consisting of
  . 30 per cent consumer products
  . 9 per cent software and services
  . 26 per cent professional products
  . 20 per cent components
  . 15 per cent non-electronic products or miscellaneous;
- a procurement of goods and services of 56 per cent of turnover;
- a wide range of cooperation, strategic alliances and joint projects, including participation in 194 European technology projects within programmes like Esprit, Race, Brite, Euram and Eureka;
- a profit after tax of Fl. 1.2 billion.

(Philips, an Industrial Company, 1891-1991; Philips Annual Reports).

Strengths and Weaknesses

During its transition to a transnational enterprise, Philips Electronics had and still has to meet the challenges and trends discussed in the previous section of this chapter.

Facing challenges is a normal activity for a company in a competitive business world. Facing challenges from a position which is evidently weak in some respects is a major problem, especially when weaknesses outnumber strengths and when threats are more numerous than opportunities.

Taking the second half of the eighties as a point of reference, the main weaknesses of Philips Electronics can be summarised as follows:

- taking into account changed exchange rates, the real market growth of the electronic industry worldwide was about 10 per cent per year. The growth of Philips turnover in the same period was about 2 per cent per year;

- often a high growth rate is accompanied by low levels of profit because of the investments needed to follow the growth of turnover. The opposite is also true in many cases. Philips however not only showed a low level of growth in turnover, but also a low level of profits. Its return on assets and its return on equity were about half of the percentages made by its main competitors;
- in a fast changing competitive environment, financial manoeuvrability is needed to be able to react at short notice. However, the liquidity of Philips, at least compared to its Japanese and US competitors, was very small;
- within Philips an impressive block of open-ended projects existed: sub-micron technology, HDTV, liquid crystal displays, interactive media, ISDN, factory automation, and so on. These projects were investments in the future of the company, but at the same time a major drain of cash and intellect;
- in a turbulent world, a company needs flexible but recognisable strategic choices or anchors to keep a sense of direction. Philips never had a tradition of setting priorities. Apart from using concepts like core business, stand alone business, new electronics businesses, niche business, portfolio choices and interlinked activities, no real choice was made in this period on the strategic direction of the company;
- the main characteristics of Philips culture in this period were: technology driven instead of market driven, functionally oriented instead of business oriented, cost optimising instead of performance optimising, defensive instead of aggressive, and regionally focused instead of globally focused.

A company like Philips, with a high turnover, a major place in important markets and a reputable performance in technology, cannot survive having just weaknesses and no strengths. The major strengths of the company can be summarised as follows:

- a presence in all geographical markets, often with organisations active in development, production, marketing and after-sales service;
- a well known and recognised broad technological base ranging from research to product development and manufacturing technology and skills;
- a traditional strength in consumer electronics, where it was one of the few to compete with the Japanese. This competitive strength was and is remarkable because not all competitors play the game by the same rules;
- a proven ability to cooperate not only with other industry partners, but also with governments. Cooperation with governments is different from cooperation with industry because of the strategic focus of the partners

involved: politics versus economics. Examples of government to industry cooperation are the sub-micron projects MEGA and JESSI, the HDTV project and many others within European programmes.

The balance of strengths and weaknesses, however, determines the capability of a company to face threats and to use the opportunities. The second half of the eighties showed clearly that for Philips Electronics, this balance was negative and even deteriorating, disadvantaging the company from facing the challenges of the nineties.

Ansoff (1984) stated that environmental turbulence had reached 9 on a scale of 10 but that the reaction of management had only reached 5 on the same scale. This statement does not seem to have lost its relevance.

Centurion Operation

In a turbulent environment a company should be headed by an entrepreneurial leadership instead of by a management. If the turbulence is not only outside the company but also inside, this leadership should be charismatic as well in order to turn around existing patterns. At the beginning of the nineties, this sort of leadership was introduced in Philips as part of a revolution named 'Centurion'. The centurion operation is not meant to be only a turn-around management manoeuvre, but also a lasting change in mindset, in organisational structure and in company direction. This is order to realise sustainable growth and the level of profitability necessary to take the opportunities, face the threats and convince all stakeholders in the company that this new situation is here to stay. This change is meant to be a strategic device that captures the essence of winning, is stable over time, and sets targets that demand personal effort and commitment (Hamel and Prahahad, 1989).

The centurion operation started in the autumn of 1990 after Philips had lost credibility with its shareholders in the preceding months. Centurion consists of two main elements: mentality and organisation.

Mentality

The mentality-changing process involves all levels in the organisation, its goal being to create a cultural break with the past by stressing basics that are common to the operation of all successful enterprises but that were less visible or invisible within Philips. The most basic idea to be communicated is that there are no guarantees for success; especially in the highly competitive environment Philips is operating in, it cannot be taken for granted that the company will survive. To many people working at Philips the possibility of failure or collapse was a cultural shock. Based upon this basic premise, other mental attitudes were introduced and communicated company-wide and interactively from top to bottom and from bottom to top. The main items of the mentality change are:

- the only way to judge performance is external benchmarking: it is not so relevant whether your business performs well according to your own standards, but whether your business performs better or worse compared with your competitors;
- the only judge of your business performance is the customer. Price/performance inclusive quality software and so on are the criteria for the customer and not technology or image;
- the people working in the company are personally accountable for living up to their own responsibilities. Everyone is personally accountable of his/her own level of responsibility and cannot hide behind the organisation as a whole or behind such so-called sacred cows as 'strategic' activities;
- every level of management in the company must aim for profitability by efficiency, simplicity, cost effectiveness and opportunity searching. This management must evince visible leadership;
- diversity in responsibilities must not lead to sub-optimisation. Consensus building is essential to safeguard coherence.

Again, these are basic elements in operating a competitive company, but were not recognised as such at all levels of Philips Electronics. Stressing these elements was a revolution to many and an excellent example of lateral thinking: always underline the necessity for creativity and personal responsibility and discard the ballast of the past (de Bono, 1987).

The Organisation
The organisational element of the centurion operation consists of two phases and four steps.

The first phase was and is the restructuring phase, its goal being to close the performance gap between Philips and its main competitors. The first step taken in this phase was the sealing of the profit leaks in integrated circuits and information systems. The second step taken and still in progress consists of reassessing the role of major stakeholders in the company and of efficiency drives. Concrete actions in this process are reduction of personnel; reducing dividend payouts to zero; reduction of stocks, of fixed assets and of debtors; and reassessing the position of creditors and of suppliers. The third step in this phase, partly belonging to the second one, is portfolio screening.

The second phase of the centurion operation is and will be focusing on a clear strategic direction and making sure that the mentality changing process and the organisational revamp pay off in profit and in the elements that create profit like customer orientation, accountability, and so on.

Of course, this organisational element of the centurion process is not revolutionary in itself. A competitive company has to restructure and revitalise continuously. Within Philips, however, many of these processes were far from automatic, so that the structured process taking place now is often considered revolutionary inside as well as outside the company.

The centurion process is not an isolated event in a standstill environment. The world inside and outside Philips keeps moving: technological progress enjoys a speed it never had before, Philips and its competitors changed their portfolios; Philips had to find an answer to its geographical imbalance, and cooperation changed the industry's landscape.

Because technological progress cannot be measured by one single yardstick, but only explained by random examples such as the processing power of microcomputers (1981 = 100, 1985 = 1000, 1990 = 50,000; European Electronic Component Manufacturers Association, 1987), the following will give more details about the other elements that continue to modify the environment of 'operation centurion'.

Philips, as well as its competitors, changed their portfolios in the past period to remedy differing growth rates in various electronics subsectors. These changes are shown in Table 5.4.

Table 5.4 Changes in portfolios of electronics companies in percentages of relevant turnovers

Some electronics companies	Consumer products		Professional products/ components		Software and services	
	1985	1991	1985	1991	1985	1991
IBM	0	0	68	57	32	43
Matsushita	65	53	35	47	0	starting
Philips	42	35	52	54	6	11
Samsung	100	59	0	41	0	0
Sony	86	64	14	15	0	21

Source: Philips annual reports 1985-1991.

Although the definition of software and services in this chart also contains entertainment and so is different from the definition used in Table 5.1, the conclusion is clear: the companies mentioned, including Philips, moved from the slow growth area of consumer products to such higher growth sectors as professional products and components, but most especially to the high growth area of software and services. Philips focused on this area, for example, by the development of Polygram NV, by its participation in Whittle Communications and in Blockbuster Entertainment and by its dramatic (very expensive because of huge hidden losses) takeover of Superclub.

Philips has had a longstanding commitment, expressed many times by its representatives, to become a balanced triangular company: an equal or at least a major presence in sales and production in the three main economic areas of the world (US, Far East, Europe).

A comparison of Philips activities between 1985 and 1991 is shown in Table 5.5. Although exchange rate fluctuations have had an important impact on the percentages presented, the general message is clear: Philips has not yet found an answer to its geographical imbalance. The company is still far from being a triangular transnational corporation. Not only is its home base Europe, but its sales and production are also concentrated in this area.

Table 5.5 Geographical imbalance of Philips activities in percentages

Areas	turnover		capital used		personnel	
	1985	1991	1985	1991	1985	1991
US/Canada	29	23	20	17	16	16
Asia	7	10	7	11	8	14
Europe	53	58	66	66	64	55
Rest of the World	11	9	7	2	12	15

Source: Philips annual reports 1985-1991.

Cooperation

Cooperation between companies and between companies and governments, aimed at reducing transaction costs by way of networking, has changed and still is changing the industry's landscape. Philips participated in and often initiated the current wave of cooperation and strategic alliances. Three main areas of cooperation can be distinguished: in pre-production, production and post-production.

1. *Cooperation and strategic alliances in pre-production*

In this area, again, three different sorts of alliances can be distinguished: cooperation with co-makers, cooperation in R&D and cooperation between industry and government on infrastructural projects.

Between 1985 and 1991, the part of purchases in total turnover of Philips increased from 53.4 per cent to 56 per cent. Within the total amount of Philips purchases, six categories are almost equal; public commodities like electricity; buildings and company infrastructure; materials; parts and components; finished products, and services. Because of efficiency drives, the first two categories have most probably shown relative decreases. If the third category has remained a constant factor, Philips must have increased its purchase percentage in areas where co-makership is an important element by about 15 per cent or Fl. 2 billion in the period 1985-1991. However, this does not mean that cooperation with co-makers has reached a level where the reduction of transaction costs by way of networking is comparable to the levels reached by important competitors like the Japanese. Many Japanese electronics companies competing on the world market against Philips add only 25 to 30 per cent own value to their turnover. Their part of purchases in total turnover is almost 50 per cent more important compared to Philips. Within this large part of purchases, the role of main suppliers is dominant in the Japanese environment. These main suppliers are larger companies that cooperate in design, production and logistics. Philips, in contrast, has many suppliers but only a few main suppliers. In Europe alone, the company purchases goods and services from about 100,000 firms, with not more than 5 per cent of this total number supplying more than Fl. 1 million. This weak supplier infrastructure is not specific to Philips, but is considered a general European problem. Meanwhile Philips is contributing to the supplier infrastructure of Europe by transforming parts of the company from internal suppliers to suppliers on the external market. Examples are the machine factories, plastics and metalware factories and the key modules group of the product division consumer electronics.

Cooperation in R&D is one of the areas of strategic alignment in which Philips is a leader. This cooperation can take many different forms, all of which are aimed at sharing risk, reducing costs and minimising development time. One way of cooperating in R&D is co-design as it is practised by the product division semi-conductors: by electronic data interchange, customer and supplier work together in the design of custom-made integrated circuits in order to share development costs and speed up the introduction of new products. Another way is cooperation in the development of world market products. Examples are the development and pilot production of very large-scale integrated circuits with SGS-Thomson Microelectronics, the development of CD-I hardware in a consortium with Matsushita and Sony, and the development of CD-I software with many companies.

Philips participation in various technology programmes must also be mentioned. Some of these were and are multinational, including the submicron MEGA project and the HDTV-programme. Others are a combination of multinational and supranational programmes like Eureka, in which Philips contributes to projects on car navigation and high power lasers. Others again are supranational programmes like Esprit, Race and Brite/Euram. Philips participates in about 20 per cent of projects within these European technology programmes. This means that Philips is one of the main contributors.

The last area of strategic alliances in pre-production is cooperation between industry and government on infrastructural innovations. Probably because of its multinational history, Philips plays an important role in this kind of networking. One example of the company's activities in this area is the DMCS900 consortium dealing with the new pan-European digital cellular network. The most important example to mention, however, is the HDTV-project in which industry and government are working together to provide an infrastructure to facilitate the introduction of this new D2-MAC and HD-MAC transmission standard. The role of Philips is dominant here.

2. *Cooperation and strategic alliances in production*

In this area, too, different sorts of alliances can be distinguished including cooperation in standards necessary for building world standards and specialisation in production and joint production. As many new products are destined for the world market, international standards are of prime importance. The lessons learned from non-standardised computer production and from the destructive effects of three different videorecorder standards have not been forgotten. Good examples of strategic alliances in standards are provided by products like the digital compact cassette (DCC) and CD-I. With regard to DCC, agreements have been reached not only with competitor-producers, but also with producers of magnetic tape and with music entertainment companies. Also for CD-I, a wide range of agreements on standards had to be negotiated with competitor-producers, producers of key modules and software producers. For one major product - HDTV - it has not been possible to negotiate international standards beyond individual geographical regions. As far as can be seen, two and possibly even three transmission standards will be used in Europe, Japan and the US respectively. Also the present PAL/SECAM and NTSC systems are different. However, the world of software production is becoming ever more international and the existence of two or three different systems will almost certainly have a negative impact on the speed with which new television opportunities embraced by these producers.

Specialisation in production is a rare phenomenon. Competition laws are of major importance here. Implicit specialisation still represents reality in various parts of the electronics industry. Examples can be found in the production of HDTV equipment, of medical equipment and of industrial electronics and the like. Because of oligopolistic markets, these specialisations are in the grey area between normal competition and the power structures that are forbidden by competition laws.

Joint production is also a rare phenomenon. In most cases these joint productions are only transitory phases between different entities producing the same sort of product and one distinct company producing these commodities. A longlasting joint production venture cannot exist except in very special arm's length circumstances. An example is the joint venture on batteries between Philips and Matsushita. In pilot productions, the early period of the transitory phase, joint productions are more common. A Philips example is liquid crystal displays (LCD).

3. *Cooperation and strategic relations in post-production*

Forward integration by way of strategic relations between producers on the one hand and distributors or stakeholders in distribution on the other, is of increasing importance in various sectors of industry. Electronics is not an exception. Philips has made and is still making efforts to strengthen its ties with co-sellers. Its participation in Superclub, Videoland, Whittle Communications and Blockbuster Entertainment are clear examples. Other instances can be found in cooperation with publishers on CD-I and in working together with Kodak and Photo-CD.

From the examples given within these three main areas of cooperation, one evident conclusion can be drawn: the closer to the market, the more competition is relevant and the more difficult cooperation and strategic alliances become Philips participation in the international wave of cooperation is no exception to this rule.

The total picture of the (r)evolution of Philips is a very complex one. In its transition to become a transnational company, Philips has had to respond to an environment changing at a fast speed while at the same time fighting a revolutionary battle within the company itself. With regard to some elements, Philips found an adequate response by following the changes in market growth in various subsectors, building large networks based on cooperation, sealing major profit leaks and reassessing the role of stakeholders in the company.

As for some other elements the outcome is less clear. An example is the attempt to change mental attitudes. This is a very delicate process and has to be built partly on trust in the future of the company. The present problems in worldwide consumer electronics markets and the profit squeeze resulting from this (in the midst of a situation where Philips has lost major financial resources in restructuring) are setbacks in this respect.

As for an element like geographical balance, no improvement can be measured. Philips is still a European-based company. In thinking about the future of the electronics industry and the future of Philips within it, this geographical focus has to be taken into account.

FUTURE

Electronics is growing so fast that within a very short period of time it will be the largest branch of industry. Also electronics is pervasive, its products penetrating other sectors and increasing their productivity, quality and flexibility. The different subsectors of the electronics industry will in future not be as separated as they have been: consumer products are penetrating the professional markets and vice versa. Also the different functions of electronic products will increasingly be integrated: communication, data processing, entertainment, information and services. Finally, the human capital intensive electronics industry will increasingly use technologies and skills outside electronics itself: chemical know-how, optical knowledge, entertainment, educational skills and so on.

In summary, if the electronics sector or even a substantial part of it is lost to a country or to a coherent geographical area, vital parts of society will become dependent on foreign suppliers and so will the possibility to self-determine the paths of economic, social and cultural growth.

Nor can it be taken for granted that the electronics industry in Europe, for instance, will take part in this future. Looking at the major competitors and the subsectors where they are active, European industry ranks in the world league only in terms of consumer products, medical electronics and to some degree in telecommunications; even in these subsectors European production is weak. Of all the major European companies, Philips Electronics is the most transnational, but even it focuses on European sales and European production. A strengthening of the European electronics industry must therefore concentrate on European companies or possibly on non-European companies that have integrated into the continental environment in such a way that they can be recognised as European.

In addition to Keynesian policies to foster and stabilise growth, future-oriented cooperation between companies and governments is the key to exploring and increasing competitive strength (Mytelka, 1991). This public-private cooperation should include numerous areas like education, R&D infrastructure, guarantees for free trade and fair competition and, last but not least, a pro-active European industrial policy consisting of a combination of push and pull projects (Porter, 1990; European Round Table of Industrialists, 1991).

Push projects are technology oriented and aimed at increasing both technological capabilities and the willingness to cooperate in research and development. These projects are rather well nurtured in Europe. Other such cooperative projects are intergovernmental, like the Mega-project between Germany and the Netherlands, aimed at increasing their technological capabilities in developing and producing submicron integrated circuits.

Pull projects are application oriented and aimed at stimulating the market-place. A pro-active European industrial policy should develop many more projects of this sort. They provide excellent opportunities to stimulate standardisation and thus create headstarts in new standardised markets. In pull projects governments (as facilitator) and industry (as supplier of products and systems) work very closely together in infrastructural projects, mostly based on more mature technologies and aiming to create opportunities for new businesses in services and technologies. Also important are demonstration projects, mostly based on emerging technologies, aimed at illustrating the usefulness of technical solutions in real environments.

In order for these pull projects to be acceptable and effective, they must be selected very carefully, selection being based on the following criteria:

. strategic importance to industry: the projects have to stimulate substantial market growth because of the possibility of their large scale application;
. fit into European political priorities: the projects have to have an enabling function in areas like education, communication, information and/or they have to be built on European R&D programmes;
. based on existing European skills and knowledge and stimulate European alliances;
. application and future oriented: the technologies (mature or emerging) have to exist, whereas application oriented European activities do not exist yet.

Apart from existing projects like HDTV, possible additional projects could include: CD-I educational tools, upgraded pan-European minitel, car navigational systems, smart card application, for instance in the complex medical environment, and so on.

A pre-condition to any future oriented policy of course is that the company should be healthy. The Philips centurion process is meant to provide an answer to this requirement.

SUMMARY

The (r)evolution of an enterprise is only partly influenced by macro-economics. The dynamics that have a major impact on the development of a company like Philips Electronics are the rapid changes in the environment and the ways such a company answers to changing circumstances.

The most important environmental changes Philips has to face are the evolution of the different subsectors in the electronics industry; the development of strengths and weaknesses in production in the different geographical regions; of increasing globalisation; of growing concentration and cooperation; of rapid advances in technology; of ever more important influence of activities at the border of the electronics sector itself, for example software; and last but not least the reactions of competitors to these changed environments.

During its transition from a multinational to a transnational enterprise, Philips has to answer to the challenges coming from outside. This answer has to be given by a company whose internal balance of strengths and weaknesses which determines the capability to face threats and use the opportunities, was negative and even deteriorating.

Philips tries to find an answer to this confrontation of external changes and internal imbalances by way of its centurion process, consisting of a (r)evolutionary mentality changing process and an also (r)evolutionary set of organisational changes. This centurion process is not a stand alone operation, but is accompanied by continuous changes in areas like technology, portfolio shifts, geographical shifts and cooperation with other enterprises and with governments.

Thus the total picture of the (r)evolution of Philips is a very complex one.

With the pre-condition that Philips wins its revolutionary internal battle, the future has more opportunities than threats however. A main element in this future is the growing recognition by governments of electronics, probably resulting in public-private cooperation including a pro-active industrial policy with a combination of push and pull projects.

APPENDIX 5.1

The EIC includes the following product categories in different electronics industries.

Data Processing	:	computers and peripherals, terminals.
Software and Services	:	systems engineering, software and packages, consulting, processing services (the new relevant subsector of educational and entertainment software is not included here).
Professional Electronics Equipment	:	mobile radio, professional radio/television, radar equipment, navigation aids, etc.
Consumer Products	:	television sets, radios, video recorders, videocameras, videodisc players, compact disk players, tape/cassettes, and so on.
Active Components	:	professional and consumer tubes, discrete semi-conductors, integral circuits.
Telecommunications	:	switches, transmission terminals.
Passive Components	:	resistors, capacitors, connectors, printed boards, etc.
Measurement/ Instrumentation	:	logic analysers, scientific measuring instruments, process control equipment, test equipment.
Automation and Industrial Processing	:	computer aided design/manufacturing, digital control systems, robots, industrial computers, industrial control equipment.
Office Automation	:	electronic typewriters, word processing systems, copiers.
Medical Electronics	:	medical imaging, pacemakers, diagnostics and monitoring systems.

REFERENCES

Annual Reports of several electronics companies, 1985-1991.
Ansoff, I. (1984), *Implanting Strategic Management*, Prentice Hall.
Commission of the European Communities (1991), *The European Electronics and Information Technology Industry*, Brussels.
de Bono, E. (1987), *Lateral Thinking for Management*, Pelican Books.
EIC, *Electronics in the World*. Paris/New York: 1991.
European Electronics Component Manufacturers Association (1987), 'An Integrated Future for Europe', *Harvard Business Review*, 69-73.

European Round Table of Industrialists (1991), *Reshaping Europe*.

Hamel, G. and C.K. Prahalad (1989), 'Strategic Intend', *Harvard Business Review*, May/June.

Hamel, G. and C.K. Prahalad (1990), 'The Core Competence of the Corporation', *Harvard Business Review*, May/June, Eindhoven: Philips International.

Mytelka, L.K. (ed) (1991), *Strategic Partnership and the World Economy: States, Firms and International Competition*. London: Pinter Publishers.

Philips Annual Reports 1985-1991.

Porter, M.E. (1980), *Competitive Strategy: Techniques for Analyzing Industries and Competitors*. New York: The Free Press.

Porter, M.E. (1985), *Competitive Advantage: Creating and Sustaining Superior Performance*. New York: The Free Press.

Porter, M.E. (1990), *The Competitive Advantage of Nations*, New York: The Free Press.

Philips (1991), *An Industrial Company, 1891-1991*.

Philips International (1989), *The European Electronics Industry*, a 'Background Paper'.

Prestowitz Jr., C.V. (1988), *Trading Places: How We allowed Japan to Take the Lead*. New York: Basic Books.

Wall Street Journal, 'Blurred Borders', 26 February 1992.

6. The Holding Company in Belgium: a Case Study of the *Société Générale*

Frans Buelens

INTRODUCTION

Classical theory assumes markets are perfect; producers are many; the objective of firms is profit maximisation, and governments behave as independent actors who do not interfere with the market process. These assumptions have time and again been questioned because of their non-realistic character with regard to capitalist society whose dominant structure is oligopoly. When observing the European scene, a typical structure of oligopolistic organisation constantly emerges; this is the holding company, which will be the subject of this chapter. Some additional empirical material with regard to the holding company in Belgium and some of the theoretical problems it poses will be highlighted in an historical perspective.

Naturally, the holding company is not an exclusively Belgian phenomenon. The same structure dominates the economy of some of the major European countries, for example Germany ('Deutsche Bank') and Sweden (the 'Wallenberg group'), whereas in other European countries it shares its influential position with other types of organisations, such as big independent firms like Fiat and Philips. By examining the Belgian case, we hope to provide insights into the way holding companies as such function (Jenkinson and Mayer, 1992).

Although there are quite a few holding companies in Belgium (for example, Almanij and GBL), we prefer to focus on just one, namely the *Société Générale*, which is the largest in the country. This method has the advantage of enabling us to investigate in depth the internal functioning of such a holding company. Although we shall begin by providing the necessary descriptive information about the holding company, the purpose of this chapter is to go beyond the descriptive level. We are, of course, well aware of the usefulness of the descriptive stage; all too often theoretical work into the theory of the firm restricts itself to some ideal types and does not fully take into account everyday realities. In general, descriptive work leads to the inevitable conclusion that a holding company indeed wields enormous power. Our contribution has a wider scope and focuses not only on the holding company's very real economic power, but also on the effective use it makes of its power with respect to influencing market outcomes. By doing this the holding company challenges traditional neoclassical theory on two counts:

1. The independent firm does not exist within the framework of a holding company; 'free' enterprise and 'free' markets are more or less a myth; since empire building is a valid long-term goal, profit maximisation is not necessarily the sole or main objective of the holding company.
2. Economic metapower (the existence of which will again be demonstrated by the case study of the *Société Générale*) can strongly influence political decision making. The question is not only what governments should do; in fact, they are already too much involved in the power game of the holding company.

In the short historical survey we will be able to elaborate on this power relationship: it will be impossible to be exhaustive here, but we hope that sufficient facts will be given to underpin our conclusion that the metapower of the holding company can considerably influence both the political decision-making process and the way decisions are taken in individual firms.

THE HOLDING COMPANY: DEFINITIONS

A 'holding company' is a company that 'holds' shares in other companies but does not exercise any industrial or financial activity of its own. One can imagine a team of investors who pool their capital in order to acquire shares in other companies with the sole objective of acquiring a high and stable return. So far this type of ownership structure resembles a simple 'investment company'. However, a holding company has a fundamental characteristic which differentiates it from a simple investment company: the holding company has the explicit objective of controlling the strategy of the companies owned. In order to achieve this, the holding company must have a substantial stake, not just hold a few equity shares. Within the legal framework of modern capitalism, it is possible to control considerable capital with a relatively small capital outlay. As a rule the acquisition of this controlling stake makes it possible for the holding company to be active in different sectors, merging the strategies of different firms into one great metastrategy which considerably enhances the power position[1] of the holding company in the economy concerned. Daems provides the following definition of control:

> Control over a company is best defined, then, as *having the control instruments* (representation on the board of directors or a 'substantial' share of equity capital) *needed to monitor capital management in a company* (Daems, 1978, p. 62).

As the above definition states it is not so easy to determine how many equity shares are needed in order to exercise control: sometimes a package of 50 per cent of equity shares is not enough to ensure full control over all the essential decisions (a blocking coalition of minority shareholders can of course be formed); sometimes a package of 10 per cent suffices to exercise control. A technique frequently used in Belgium is 'cross-participation': the mother company holds share packages in the daughter companies and vice versa. A further distinction can be made regarding the degree of dependence: sometimes control of a given company is shared by two or more holding companies.

The holding company as such can be considered as a special but frequently occurring case of the network system (Fennema, 1982). Whereas control over a wide diversity of industries can be acquired because one particular industrial company is very powerful, the typical European holding company owes its existence to banking capital. Originally banks took shares in industrial firms. The Belgian holding company developed out of the Belgian banking system which at first did not separate its banking activities from its holding activities. In the years 1934-1935 this separation did take place, whereas in a country like Germany it was not effected.[2] Thus, in a broad sense the field of investigation includes the 'mixed bank' ('Universalbanken').

In fact, the mixed banking system had opted for dangerous practices in what is, after all, a very important sector of the economy: short-term deposits were transformed into long-term investment in industry. This kind of practice may lead to the collapse of the financial system. Not only can the bank not protect the companies it controls in a time of severe crisis, but the system can also be a threat to the bank itself. Consequently, government intervention in Belgium in the thirties forced the separation of banking from industrial activities, whereas in other countries banking was very strictly regulated. From that time the bank acquired a certain independence and autonomy, although the holding company continued to hold bank shares.

The holding company system thus has a certain historical origin, but many organisational structures have developed along the same lines and have the same essential characteristics. Our definition of the holding company differs from that of Williamson who described it as 'a loosely divisionalised structure in which the controls between the headquarters unit and the separate operating parts are limited and often unsystematic' (Williamson, 1986, p. 61). The Williamson six-way classification scheme (Williamson, 1986, pp. 69-70) is a useful contribution to the classification of large corporate structures, but does not fully take into account historically based realities of the holding concept in Europe. Our study states that the SG holding company in fact represents more than 'a corporate shell' (Williamson, 1986, p. 153) and has much more of the Williamsonian 'M form conglomerate' (Williamson, 1985, p. 288). Using his classification we prefer to make use of the term 'conglomerate' to identify the nine largest European groups of this type (Table 6.1). Conglomerates (industrial-centred, bank-centred or family-centred (Kester, 1992, p. 29)) which control a number of different activities are on the rise in every developed industrial country. It is not so much their historical origin as their formal structure which is important, although the method of historical analysis of capitalist institutions is a necessary step to provide additional material to answer theoretical questions. In this way the study of the holding company can clarify practices of different types of economic power concentrations.

Table 6.1 The nine largest European conglomerates

Place in FT top-100 (1991)	Market Capitalisation (billion $)
9 Deutsche Bank	20,9
11 Hanson	19,6
13 BAT Industries	17,-
21 BTR	12,6
37 Suez	9,3
52 Paribas	7,6
58 Procardia	7,3
69 Generale Maatschappij	6,0
92 Volvo	4,6

Source: Financial Times

THE HOLDING COMPANY: A RESEARCH AGENDA

The research agenda need not only take into account the economic power position, although much of the work on holding companies has focused on just this aspect: it has been demonstrated with different kinds of techniques that a huge concentration of power can be measured. This is the real background of some of the empirical work that has been done, for example, by the CRISP research centre which has investigated formal control participations between holding companies and subsidiaries, the kind of study which provides striking evidence (CRISP, 1966; Vincent, 1990). Some other research has been concluded on interlocking directories (Cuyvers and Meeusen, 1976; Daems, 1978; Fennema, 1982). All these different approaches have one thing in common: they all arrive at the conclusion that an enormous concentration of economic power really does exist. In this respect two relations are important: first, the relation of the holding company with the firms it dominates and, second, the relation of the holding company with political institutions.

The firm as such, the independent autonomous unit, does not exist within the holding company. Resource allocation processes are no longer a matter for the firm itself, but are decided upon at the holding company level; the 'transfer price' system as observed within a multinational can be applied to the holding company as well: profits can be shifted from one company to another; firms can be forced to go bankrupt or to stop their activities, and investments are not mainly for economic reasons. Similarly, massive financial means (extracted from other companies) may be concentrated in a few sectors in which the holding company wants to build up a strong position. None of the firms controlled by the holding company still follows an independent strategy; the strategy is defined at the headquarters of the holding company and reflects the interests of the dominant group in this kind of network, all too often disregarding the interests of other groups such as minority shareholders and employees. The result is a network of firms without autonomous decision-making power since all of them are subjected to the metastrategy of the mother company.

There is not only a relation between mother and daughter companies but also a relation between the metapower of the holding company and political power.[3] A holding company exercises considerable influence on the decision-making processes of governments. Following the public choice approach of Olson (1965), governmental decisions are influenced by pressure groups. Those pressure groups with almost unlimited financial means will exert a great influence. It will be demonstrated later that different examples overwhelmingly support Olson's thesis: the holding company indeed exerts enormous influence on political decisions in the country. This also makes the holding company as such a controversial institution (FGTB, 1956; Cottenier, 1989). In a democratic society it is assumed that power lies with parliament and with a democratically elected government. However, too many facts indicate that real power all too often lies in the hands of holding companies.

THE *SOCIÉTÉ GÉNÉRALE*: A BRIEF HISTORICAL SURVEY

The holding company is deeply rooted in capitalist society. In some European countries economic development was stimulated in the 19th century by government helping to raise banking capital. This type of development was typical of, for example, in Sweden, Germany and Belgium (Kindleberger, 1984).

The *Société Générale* (SG) was founded as a bank ('Société Générale des Pays-Bas pour favoriser l'industrie nationale'; 'Algemeene Nederlandsche Maatschappij ter begunstiging van de volksvlijt')[4] in 1822 by the Dutch King William I, who provided most of the capital. The explicit objective was to develop national industry which was starting up on the continent at the time. (After Belgian independence shares were transferred to Belgian owners.) Developing industries were funded by means of banking capital, as the necessary capital could not be raised by private persons. First came infrastructure, then the key sectors of industrial development; the SG invested heavily in coal mining and the steel industry. Later the holding company invested in a series of metallic industries. The bank also provided funds for independent firms. When the firms in situations of recession were unable to pay off their debts, the SG became the owner of their equity shares. Thus the empire grew until it soon controlled large parts of the structure of the Belgian economy (steel, coal, electricity, paper, cement, banking, insurance, glass, heavy transportation, textiles). Until 1850 the bank played the role of central bank in the country (Generale Maatschappij, 1972).

A decisive impetus was given by the colonisation period. Belgium (as other European countries) took part in the occupation of large parts of Africa, the most important being the Congo region in Central Africa (the present Zaïre). Stimulated by the Belgian King Leopold II (who was condemned at the time by the international community for the extreme brutality of his colonial exploitation), the SG very soon became interested in the natural resources of the colony. It founded a daughter company, the 'Union Minière du Haut Katanga', for the exploitation of the mines (1906) and several other companies for the exploitation of diamonds (Sibeka) and natural resources.

To facilitate transportation of these colonial products to the mother country, the CMB ('Compagnie Maritime Belge') was founded; ships were built in the Antwerp region (Cockerill Yards) and the port of Antwerp flourished thanks to the increase in the trade of colonial products. Minerals were extracted and exported to Belgium where they were upgraded in newly-built plants such as 'Métallurgie'. Belgium's comparative advantage in these sectors was mainly due to its colonial possessions. The structure of the colonial economy depended on the interest it held for the development of the Belgian economy. For example, one of the few railways constructed in the colonies was the 'Benguela railway': its function was to connect the mineral-rich region of Katanga with the nearest harbour in Angola. The economy of the colony became closely linked to that of Belgium. Belgian industry founded affiliated companies in the colony whenever it was necessary to exploit mineral and agricultural resources.

When the Congo became independent in 1960 the holding company[5] forced the Belgian government to protect its interests in the former colony. In 1961 it favoured the secession of the rich mining province of Katanga, and in 1965 it supported the Mobutu dictatorship of the country. In 1967 the mining activities were nationalised: the 'Union Minière' (daughter of the SG) was promised massive compensation (between BEF 41.5 billion and BEF 50.2 billion (Verhaeren, 1972, pp. 371-374).[6]

In 1981 a fundamental restructuring process began in order to adapt the SG to new realities; this process was interrupted by the takeover by Suez (1988).

THE *SOCIÉTÉ GÉNÉRALE*: A BRIEF LOOK AT THE STRUCTURE OF THE HOLDING COMPANY

Before discussing further developments, it may be useful to provide a short survey of the enormous variety of activities conducted by the holding company (Figure 6.1). We have opted to present the structure of the SG just before its takeover by the holding company Suez. This overview indicates the power structure which linked these different fields of activity (more than 1200 companies!). It is obvious that the SG played a major role in banking, insurance and energy provision in Belgium and that it exerted considerable influence in other sectors. As Figure 6.1 indicates the SG had strong positions before the Suez takeover in finance and insurance (Tanks, GIF, Sodecom, Generale Bank, AG, Royale Belge); electricity (Ebes, Intercom, Unerg); petroleum (Petrofina); engineering (Tractebel); non-ferro (Union Minière); cement (CBR); transport (CMB); diamonds (Sibeka); chemicals (Gechem); trading (Generale Trading); steel (Arbed, Sidmar); arms (FN, PRB); real estate (IVB) and the paper industry (Pabeltec).

Figure 6.1 *Companies in which the Société Générale held an interest (as of 31 December 1987)*

Name of the company	(I)	(II)	(III)
Tanks	140 GBP (c)	100.00%	-
GIF, Luxemburg	2.255 (1)	97.50%	2.50%
Coördin. Centrum 'Generale'	2.096	100.00%	-
Sodecom	2.029	33.33%	66.67%
Generale Bank (*)	48.986 (c)	13.82%	0.06%
VIV	671 (3)	35.85%	29.95%
Synerfi	350 (4)	37.00%	30.00%
AG Groep (*)	15.286 (c)	13.83%	8.23%
Royale Belge (*)	34.332 (c)	2.50%	7.61%
Assubel-Leven (*)	1.762	8.43%	1.83%
Tractebel	53.098 (c)	15.59%	18.04%
CEDEE	10	40.00%	25.00%
Electrafina	9.965	26.00%	0.10%
Belgatel	10.700 (2)	25.00%	25.00%
Havas (*)	1.361 FRF (c)	5.00%	-
Union Minière	18.924 (c)	100.00%	-
CBR	13.455 (c)	37.92%	0.27%
CMB	6.590 (c)	46.93%	5.43%
Sibeka	5.380	54.22%	-
Gechem	1.463 (c)	51.56%	0.94%
Generale Trading Cy.	4.505 (c)	46.38%	48.75%
Sofina	16.399 (c)	25.25%	0.89%
Finoutremer	2.129 (2)	39.23%	-
Suez (*)	18.786 FRF (c)	1.54%	-
Arbed (*)	24.124 LUF	24.70%	0.15% (5)
CFE	4.223 (c)	24.51%	-
CGE	16.022 FRF (c)	1.79%	-
FN	1.624 (c)	50.11%	0.03%
Immob. Vennoot. van België	3.281 (c)	20.29%	1.89%
Pabeltec	3.280 (c)	24.00%	5.69%

For every company the following figures are given:
- total shareholders' equity (I) (in millions) at the end of 1987; (c) when consolidated figures are available
- direct (II) and indirect (III) percentages held by the SG
(*) not controlled (i.e. other majority shareholder)
(1) 31.3.88 (2) 30.6.87 (3) 30.9.87 (4) 27.4.87 (5) Percentage of voting shares

Source: Generale Maatschappij, Annual Report, 1987, p. 21.

The structure of the holding company indicates that in some of these sectors it almost held a monopoly position. For example, in one of the key sectors of any economy, that of electricity, it had acquired a monopoly; until 1990 the sector formally consisted of three firms (Ebes, Intercom, Unerg) but all were controlled by the SG. In 1990 they were united in one large company: Electrabel.

In other sectors the holding company tried to exert cartelistic behaviour. In the banking sector, for example, a virtual cartel existed until recently, with nearly no price competition (fixed and relatively low interest levels).

THE HOLDING COMPANY AND THE STATE

So far we have dealt with the structure and the history of the holding company; day-to-day practice provides further evidence as to how a holding company actually works. The nature of industrial networks can be immensely clarified when such day-to-day facts (not all of them can be treated here, of course) are investigated. In this section we will focus on the connection between the government and the holding company. Obviously this relation is two-sided: the government tries to influence the behaviour of the holding company (for example, when the SG abandoned the coal sector, it was forced to promise new investments); however, the more important form of influence is that of the holding company on the government.

Using Public Finances for Private Purposes

As was stated above we will give some evidence here on how a holding company can use the government's public finance for its private objectives, thus placing a heavy financial burden on the state. The steel industry is a good example.

When the steel crisis hit the world economy in 1974, prices fell sharply and many companies made heavy losses. The crisis hit the SG in one of its key activities. At the time the holding company controlled the Cockerill-Ougrée-Providence-Espérance-Longdoz steel works in the southern part of Belgium and, together with the Luxemburg government, it also controlled Arbed which possessed the Sidmar Steel company at Zelzate (Flandres). While the Cockerill steel works incurred heavy losses, the Sidmar steel operations made profits thanks to its modern installations and its proximity to the sea. The Belgian banks, which had huge credits outstanding in the steel industry (more than BEF 100 billion), obtained from the government that it would guarantee all such credits. In 1981 the government became the owner of the loss-making Hainaut- Sambre steel works (formerly Cockerill) by transforming bank credits into capital equity.

Thus the SG got rid of loss-making parts of the industry (that had been profitable for many years), but continued to control Arbed and Sidmar; in the future, state public finance had to carry the resulting heavy burden. But that was not all: the Sidmar steel works received compensation for this subsidisation of the Southern part of the country. The government converted debts amounting to BEF 11.2 billion into equity shares (without voting rights), while considerable amounts of capital (BEF 8.3 billion) were given as compensation for government investment in the Walloon steel industry. This was possible due to the specific situation of the Belgian state with its two communities. Thanks to this massive injection of state capital, the Sidmar company realised a considerable diversification (Sidel, Sidinvest) and internationalisation (Brazil).

The same process had already been observed when the SG wanted to pull out of the coal mines in Limburg. In 1967 an agreement was reached between the Belgian state and the coal companies. The SG was allowed to divide its activities: the loss-making mines were nationalised; other intrinsically very profitable activities continued to be privately owned, for example, real estate (Goossens, 1972, pp. 382-385).

The Eurosystem Case

In 1976 the SG was involved in what became known as the Eurosystem Débâcle: The Saudi Arabian government wanted to conclude a contract for the construction of two military hospitals (BEF 36 billion). A consortium led by a daughter of the SG ('Eurosystem Hospitalier') succeeded in obtaining the contract by ousting its British and American competitors. The SG used all sorts of methods: even the Belgian prince Albert joined the efforts of the SG to obtain the contract, his visit to Saudi-Arabia being an important element in gaining Saudi confidence. An amount of BEF 8.5 billion commission fees and a 'call-girl network' were also thrown to clinch the contract. These practices only came to light in 1979 when the Eurosystem company failed.

How Fiscal losses Amounting to BEF 10 Billion can be Deducted

In 1988 the merger of two totally different companies of the holding company took place: 'ACEC' and 'Union Minière'. The reason was simply that ACEC had made great losses whereas Union Minière had made great profits! Belgian law makes it possible to deduct losses made in the previous year from profits made in the present year. To do this profits and losses have to be made within the same company. Since this was not the case the holding company constructed a merger plan. According to representatives of the holding company it was the Belgian government itself which suggested that the holding company, should exploit the Belgian tax system as fully as possible to its own advantage. Consequently, ACEC-Union Minière deducted fiscal losses amounting to BEF 10 billion from the profits of Union Minière after the merger. This complex procedure was the result of a secret deal between the tax administration and the holding company and was condoned by the government.

THE HOLDING COMPANY IN A DYNAMIC PERSPECTIVE. ADAPTING TO THE NEW ENVIRONMENT OF THE EIGHTIES: MEANS AND OBJECTIVES

Until now we have stressed the importance of the SG's power position; nevertheless this position is never an absolute one. Even extremely powerful organisations continue to depend on market processes and changes in the economic and technological climate. Their power is relative. The rapidly changing circumstances of the 1980s highlighted the weaker sides of the SG.

The SG's main interests were in some of the formerly 'basic' industrial sectors (cement, steel, coal and the like), but were absent in the new sectors. In the 1980s the comparative advantage of highly industrialised countries was shifting rapidly towards sectors in which new technologies were used. However, the SG had not invested in new sectors and was not adapted to the internationalisation process that had begun to characterise the world economy. Although the SG was well aware of this (in 1971 governor Max Nokin of the SG declared 'Nous voulons devenir une des grandes organisations multinationales du futur', see Carton, 1972, p. 408), no concrete measures were taken to cope with change.

In 1981 - under the leadership of R. Lamy, the new governor - a new effort was made to adapt the holding company: a strategic plan ('SG Futurs') was adopted in 1984. During the years 1980-1987 ambitious plans were conceived: all of the SG participants (more than 1200) were regrouped into ten key sectors. The SG wanted to become a leader in every key sector according to the following strategy:

1. The holding company wanted to become an international company (for example, the cement division (CBR) bought itself into half of the North American market).
2. The holding company wanted to invest in such new sectors as international trading, telecommunication, media and information (for example, the SG bought a minority share of 6 per cent in Alcatel for a total of BEF 10 billion).
3. The holding company wanted to consolidate its position in sectors already under its control (non-ferro, electricity, petroleum, cement, transport, finance, diamonds, chemicals).

To realise these plans the SG used two different and very important means to increase its financial possibilities: first, it made use of state finance; second, it mobilised much of its internal financial resources.

The SG lobbied very hard to obtain some state support for its recapitalisation plans. Two fundamental measures were taken by the Belgian government during the eighties. Firstly, the law 'Cooreman-Declercq' was accepted (1982) which made it possible to finance equity increases by private investors who were allowed fiscal advantages when subscribing to them. A large part of the new capital increase was issued by holding companies and companies in their sphere of influence. The SG holding company increased its capital from 9 billion BEF (1980) to 110 billion BEF (1990) (Table 6.2). Secondly, the Belgian government allowed the creation of 'coordination centres' (1982, Royal Decree, Nr. 187); companies were virtually exempted from tax provided that they fulfilled certain requirements (Van den Bulcke and de Lombaerde, 1992). The SG eagerly participated. Several subsidiaries founded 'coordination centres' which allowed them to centralize the activities of their companies so as to finance them with credits. This kind of 'fiscal paradise' in the heart of the European Community was a great success, but came in for severe criticism from other countries.

These measures had considerable influence on state finance: while contributing to the financial health of the holding company and other companies, they exacerbated the precarious position of Belgian state finances.

Not only was state finance used, in fact, but a holding company was also able to use its internal structure to finance its recapitalisation. The most striking example of this was the acquisition in 1981 of Union Minière as a 100 per cent daughter company. The latter possessed considerable funds thanks to compensation paid for the loss of its colonial possessions in 1967; those funds were captured by the SG.

Table 6.2 Capital increase of the SG

	TOTAL SHAREHOLDERS' EQUITY (millions BEF)	NUMBER OF SHARES
1980	9,472	5,802,000
1981	26,011	11,129,000
1982	26,873	10,789,000
1983	34,788	16,050,000
1984	39,842	19,310,000
1985	45,529	21,810,000
1986	52,810	24,041,000
1987	67,556	28,158,000
1988	104,777	64,059,000
1989	109,390	64,059,000
1990	110,013	64,059,000

Source: Annual Reports 'Société Générale'.

THE SUEZ TAKEOVER OF 1988: THE EUROPEAN HOLDING COMPANY, THE SG AND INTERNATIONAL STRATEGIES

After the Second World War, economic and political power was redistributed; the US became the only market economy giant and began a struggle with its main rival, the Soviet Union. European countries united. At first this process was stimulated by the US in view of its struggle against Moscow; later the process towards greater unity produced a rival to the US itself, just as had happened with Japan. The 1992 Single Market was inspired by European companies who wanted to be competitive in the Triad. The 1986 European Act had similarly been a direct consequence of pressure exerted by the European Round Table. In the new international climate it became obvious that European companies were trying to realise a greater concentration in order to be able to compete with their US and Japanese rivals (Dekker et al., 1991; De Carmoy, 1988).

One of the most important steps to date towards greater concentration in Europe was the acquisition of the SG in 1988 by the French holding company SUEZ, which resulted in a European holding company. The takeover fight was an excellent illustration of the 'casino-mentality' developed during the eighties. The period under investigation is interesting because once again some striking facts can be observed.

At the end of 1987 and during the first months of 1988 the SG was the scene of a battle between two groups: the French Suez and the Italian de Benedetti (Cerus, Olivetti) group. The Italian group launched the first takeover bid, which was immediately blocked by the Belgian Bank Commission; in the meantime the SG sought an alliance with the French Suez holding company. The SG increased its capital, and equity shares were placed with Sodecom, a subsidiary. The bidding - although not officially sanctioned - continued: the offer went from BEF 4000 to BEF 8000 per share. Finally Suez, together with allied Belgian companies such as AG Insurance, won the fight. On 14 April 1988, ownership of SG shifted to the French group.

During the Suez takeover fight with de Benedetti, the Belgian government intervened in accordance with the SG's wishes; in fact, the government acted almost as a political subsidiary of the SG. This can be shown in the way SG used the 'capital allowed clause', in the way SG financed new equity shares and, finally, in the way the government prevented de Benedetti from realising the takeover.

At the annual General Assembly of 26 August 1987, the SG included a clause in its statutes ('capital allowed') which permitted it to increase its capital by BEF 20 billion at any moment. In the general context of the raider movement in the early eighties. The intention of this clause was to enable the company to protect itself against raiders. When de Benedetti attacked, the SG immediately invoked its 'capital allowed' clause and took steps to generate 16 million shares. Ironically, a few months earlier, AG, the largest insurance company in the country and related to SG, had launched an attack on the insurance company Assubel. When the latter tried to invoke the same 'capital allowed' clause, the court refused permission.

The SG's invocation of the 'capital allowed' clause was seriously questioned by de Benedetti. A lower court, that is the Brussels Commercial Court, ruled against invocation of the clause. But the Banking Commission (after consultation with the government) gave its approval. In both cases, the same law was applied, but to different effect, and each time in favour of SG's interests!

As the new equity shares were finally issued, the SG used its control of the 'Generale Bank' to finance them in a way which goes against the spirit of the splitting of the mixed banks (see note 5). The government never intervened to curtail this technique. There are two elements to newly issued equity shares: the nominal price and the issue premium. According to Belgian law only 25 per cent of the nominal price needs to be paid, whereas the issue premium has to be paid in total. The new SG shares were given a nominal price of BEF 1252 per share; the issue premium amounted to BEF 2098 per share. The total value of a new share was then BEF 3350. Moreover, an increase in capital is allowed only when the necessary amount is readily available. The SG used the following procedure: the majority of new shares were placed by its daughter company Sodecom. The whole operation was financed by short-term credits from the 'Generale Bank' totalling over BEF 26 billion.

This practice was used before, in October 1987, when a SG capital enhancement process was started. Due to the Wall Street crash the SG did not succeed in issuing the new equity shares. The Bank then had to take over 560,000 shares and sold them at great loss (half a billion Belgian francs).

The bid by de Benedetti was ruled out almost directly by the Banking Commission, which has to give its approval before a public takeover bid can be made, with a final decision postponed until later.

In the meantime Suez entered the ring and made its own bid. As soon as almost all the shares had disappeared from the stock exchange floor, the Banking Commission approved the de Benedetti takeover bid.

HOW A MOTHER BECOMES A DAUGHTER: AFTER THE SUEZ TAKEOVER

The takeover required enormous funds from Suez, which were generated by issuing new equity shares. From then on strategic decisions relating to SG would be taken in the Suez headquarters. Two main strategies were followed.

As Suez had to pay dearly to acquire control of the SG, it engaged in the traditional asset-stripping of a raider company. Moreover it took possession of all the money available in daughter companies. In April 1991, for example, Suez demanded that the SG should pay BEF 25 billion by the end of the year. In other words, the subsidiaries of the SG had to bear the cost of the takeover fight: funds available in subsidiaries had to be used to satisfy shareholders of Suez. A few examples can be cited:

- The Sibeka participation in the SG was shifted to the ACEC-Union Minière subsidiary for BEF 6.9 billion.
- Finoutremer, a daughter company of the SG, had acquired liquidities and was obliged to transfer them to the SG in lieu of some shares in other SG subsidiaries (BEF 2.5 billion; 1991).
- Participants in Fibelpar and IVB ('Immobiliënvennootschap van België') were sold to the daughter company Tractebel (1991) for BEF 6.6 billion.

The general strategy underlying these operations has no rationale from the viewpoint of sound management; such shares do not bring any additional value. However, they do make the subsidiaries concerned more vulnerable as they no longer have any financial backing in the case of cyclical movements.

The subsidaries of the SG thus not only had to bear the cost of the takeover fight, but also still have to provide the funds needed for the strategic plans of the mother. The strategic conception of Suez differs from that of the SG. Whereas the SG can be considered as an industrial holding company, Suez is almost exclusively active in non-industrial sectors. At one time the objective of the SG was to form an industrial empire; now it is forced to concentrate its efforts on making as much money as possible. A basic characteristic of industrial activity is its cyclical dependence. Investors interested in stable dividends do not normally opt for this kind of activity. Suez is such an investor; it is thus probable that many industrial companies will be sold. In fact the process has already started (CMB, Alcatel, FN, CFE). Suez is also interested in particular kinds of participation such as tourism and finance and can use the means of its daughter companies to co-finance them (the SG invested heavily in, for example, Accor). This policy has aroused deep resentment on the part of trade unions, among others::

La stratégie du holding se pratique en termes de rentabilité financière au détriment d'une réelle politique industrielle ... les syndicats estiment que la Générale est loin d'être devenue le holding européen à stratégie industrielle que Suez prétendait vouloir former (Capron, 1991, p. 25).

CONCLUSION

So far the issue of the holding company on a European level has received little serious attention. However, like the 'Keiretsu' in Japan, it is a key element in the economic organisation in Europe. While many aspects can be studied and a lot of work has been done both in the descriptive field and in considering the extent to which a holding company controls its subsidiaries, we have focused in this chapter on the uses the holding company makes of its power. A holding company exerts considerable influence over its daughters and over the political decision makers, and attempts to use state funds whenever possible. As the holding company generally exerts control in key sectors of the economy (for example, in transport, finance, insurance and energy), it is of the utmost importance to understand the crucial role it plays in any country's economy. The question of power appears to be central in the economic organisation debate. Following the public choice approach it has to be concluded that economic metapower and the holding company in particular do influence decision making at the economic and political levels in society, one of the most visible indications of this being the personal ties which help in meshing together the two levels. With Daems we conclude that:

> The first and most important (question) has to do with shaping a public policy toward the large holding companies (Daems, 1978, p. 138).

NOTES

1. For a discussion of the power versus influence concept, see Helmers *et al.* (1975, p. 487).
2. In Germany the study focused on the concept 'Finanzkapital' (Gerhards, 1982, p. 272).
3. The kind of influence varies: personal interests are but one example. Very often influential people within the SG become members of government. The Belgian minister W. De Clercq, for example, was on the board of directors of several SG subsidiaries. Officials are also frequently found on the holding's board of directors after ending their official political mandate. EC Commissioner E. Davignon (who worked out the steel plan) became a senior member of the SG-executive (see Van Outrive 1972, pp. 422-426 and De Preter, 1983).
4. The name in French was shortened to *Société Générale* in 1830; after 1975 the holding company again had a Dutch name, that is *Generale Maatschappij*. Henceforth we will use the abbreviation SG.
5. In 1934-1935 the *Société Générale* was divided into a holding and a banking company.
6. '.. la nouvelle 'Union Minière', selon l'accord du 25 septembre 1969, percevra par l'intermédiaire de la Société Générale des Minerais (S.G.M.), une indemnité de 6 p.c. de la valeur de la production katangaise de Gecomin durant quinze ans et 1 p.c. durant encore dix ans' (Verhaeren, 1972, p. 371).

REFERENCES

Belgisch Staatsblad (1983), *Koninklijk Besluit no. 187 betreffende de oprichting van coördinatie-centra*, 13 januari, 502-510.

Capron, M. (1991), 'Le Canal de Suez', *La Revue Nouvelle*, XCIV (9), Sept., 21-25.

Carton, A. (1972), 'La Société Générale vue par la presse financière internationale', *La Revue Nouvelle*, LVI (11), Nov., 406-412.

Cottenier, J. *et al.* (1989), *De Generale 1822-1992*. Berchem: Epo.

CRISP (1966), *Morphologie des groupes financiers*, Brussels.

Cuyvers, L. and W. Meeusen (1976), 'The Structure of Personal Influence of the Belgian Holding Companies', *European Economic Review*, 8 (1), June, 51-69.

Daems, H. (1978), *The Holding Company and Corporate Control*. Leiden/Boston: Martinus Nijhoff.

De Carmoy, H. (1988), *Stratégie bancaire, le refus de la dérive*. Paris: PUF.

Dekker, W., P. Gyllenhammar and J. Monod (1991), *Reshaping Europe. A Report from the European Round Table of Industrialists*, Brussels.

De Preter, R. (1983), *De 200 rijkste families*. Berchem: Epo.

Fennema, M. (1982), *International Networks of Banks and Industry*. Ph.D. thesis, Amsterdam: University of Amsterdam.

FGTB (1956), *Holdings et Democratie Economique*. Brussels.

Generale Maatschappij (1972), *Société Générale de Belgique 1822-1972*. Brussels.

Gerhards, M. (1982), *Industriebeziehungen der westdeutschen Banken*. Frankfurt am Main: Sendler Verlag.

Goossens, P. (1972), 'La Société Générale et la KS', *La Revue Nouvelle*, LVI (11), Nov., 382-385.

Helmers *et al.* (1975), *Graven naar macht. Op zoek naar de kern van de Nederlandse Economie*. Amsterdam: Van Gennep.

Jenkinson, T. and C. Mayer (eds.) (1992), 'Corporate Governance and Corporate Control', *Oxford Review of Economic Policy*, 8 (3), Autumn.

Kester, W.C. (1992), 'Industrial Groups as systems of contractual governance', *Oxford Review of Economic Policy*, 8 (3), Autumn, 24-43.

Kindleberger, C.P. (1984), *A Financial History of Western Europe*. London: George Allen & Unwin.

Olson, M. (1965), *The Logic of Collective Action*. Cambridge/Mass.: Harvard University Press.

Société Générale de Belgique (1966-1991), *Annual Reports*.

Van den Bulcke, D. and Ph. de Lombaerde, *The Belgian Metalworking Industries and the Large European Internal Market: the Role of Multinational Investment*. CIMDA, Discussion Paper 1992/E/5.

Van Outrive, L. (1972), 'Hommes et groupes de la Société Générale et rôles publics', *La Revue Nouvelle*, LVI (11), Nov., 422-426.

Verhaeren, R.E. (1972), 'La Société Générale et l'Union Minière', *La Revue Nouvelle*, LVI (11), Nov., 371-374.

Vincent, A. (1990), *Les Groupes d'Entreprises*. Brussels: CRISP.

Williamson, O.E. (1985), *The Economic Institutions of Capitalism. Firms, Markets, Relational Contracting*. London: Macmillan.

Williamson, O.E. (1986), *Economic Organisation. Firms, Markets and Policy Control*. Brighton: Wheatsheaf Books.

7. Policy Implications of Industrial Transformation

Jan Donders and Eric van Kooij

INTRODUCTION

Market economies all over the world are undergoing industrial transformations. These transformations are mainly spurred by the advance of global competition and technological innovation. Changes taking place in the international political and economic environment of these economies are also influential. This situation has given rise to national debates on government policy towards strategic industries. These debates are often characterised by the tendency to measure the economic performance of a nation by the success or failure of local firms engaged in global competition. The main focus, hereby, is on high tech industries. Authorities in charge of industrial policy are being challenged to review their former policies. If necessary they will have to build a new industrial policy structure which can respond to current realities.

The Netherlands does not differ in this sense from other market economies in the world. In the first place, the fact that the scale of a few of the so-called Dutch 'crown jewels' of industry Volvo Car and Fokker has recently appeared to be too small to counter the hardships that come with global competition (as a result of which the control over these firms has passed to foreign hands), has increased the scrutiny directed at industrial policy. The focus is thus on the requirements industrial policy should meet in order to keep high tech, up-graded, industrial activities in our country. The purport of the argument is that the preservation of these industrial centres of excellence in The Netherlands will be at stake if they are left to the fate of foreign control. In the second place, industrial policy has attracted attention as a result of the effects of the global economic recession on certain industrial sectors.

In this chapter we will elaborate on the policy implications of industrial transformation in the sense of structural adjustment. We will therefore not dwell upon conjunctural matters. First we will give some theoretical background concerning industrial policy. We will then identify attitudes towards industrial policy in The Netherlands. This will be followed by a brief review of our post-war economic situation, an historical analysis which shows a shift in the attention given to industrial policy. Moreover, it will be shown that industrial transformation appears to have influenced the character of industrial policy.

THEORETICAL BACKGROUND OF INDUSTRIAL POLICY

Nearly every country in the world needs a strong industrial and technological base to be able to guarantee sustainable economic development. This premise presumably, does not elicit strong differences of opinion which do, however, exist when the extent of government intervention in markets is at stake. The debate then focuses on how the government intervenes and for what purposes.

Concerning the justification of industrial policy as such, two extreme points of view can be distinguished (Johnson, 1982, p. 19). On the one hand, we have the opponents of industrial policy. They argue that resources will naturally find their way into the most profitable and socially desirable uses. Government, in this view, should restrict itself to a 'market rational orientation', concerning itself solely with the forms and procedures of economic competition. Government should not determine which industries ought to exist and which are no longer needed. The United States is a good example of this first line of thought. On the other hand, we have the proponents of industrial policy. Who argue that government should promote that structure of domestic industry which enhances the nation's international competitiveness. This can be referred to as the 'plan-rational orientation'. From this perspective, economic vitality depends on the performance of dynamic sectors of the economy where it is most important that comparative advantage be created. Japan is a good example illustrating this second set of attitudes.

Now let us assume that there is a role for government to play as far as industrial policy is concerned. So we are somewhere on the continuum between the two extremes. We can then adhere to the justification and the formulation of policies which have been derived from theoretical and empirical insights contributed by 'industrial economics' (George and Joll, 1981). Mainstream industrial economics is focused on the analysis of competitive conditions, such as market structure, conduct and performance, and the advancement of normative policies such as how to improve economic prosperity and welfare. But industrial economics itself is divided into two schools of thought: the more traditional theories of 'industrial organisation' and the more recent theories of 'industrial dynamics' (Carlsson, 1989, pp. 1-3).

In industrial organisation, individual firms are regarded as responsible for economic vitality. According to this view vitality is determined by competition between firms. Government therefore should safeguard this competition. At the same time, however, the existence of market failures justifies government intervention. Large fixed costs of entry, substantial economies of scale, steep learning curves with potential spillovers across firms, as well as imperfections in capital and product markets stemming from asymmetries of information are considered to be the market distortions which can be corrected by targeted policy tools. For example, in the case of steep learning curves with potential spillovers across firms, the internalisation of positive external effects can be achieved by giving subsidies for R&D. Or in the case of imperfections in capital markets, government can offer credit facilities for technological development. With industrial organisation, these policy tools are always directed at individual firms.

In industrial dynamics, however, economic vitality is determined by the institutional setting in which firms operate. Gaining dynamic increasing returns depends on this setting. Strategic advantages of long-term access to certain products and technologies, the early selection of industrialisation locations and essential forward and backward linkages in terms of material and knowledge inputs and outputs favour strategic policies (Soete, 1991, pp. 54-57). For example, in the case of essential forward and backward linkages, mutual cooperation between individual firms and between firms and other actors, such as research centres, can be stimulated by giving subsidies to cooperative R&D projects. Or in the case of cumulative learning and dynamic increasing returns associated with technological advance, government can support the R&D of highly pervasive technologies. With industrial dynamics the main interest is in causal chains, namely in disequilibria and chain effects created *inter alia* by entrepreneurial activities, market processes and competition as a dynamic force (Dahmen, 1984, p. 25).

The distinction between industrial organisation and industrial dynamics is very theoretical and one rather hard to maintain in the everyday reality of policy making. The general conceptions of this distinction, however, give us enough foothold to be able to review industrial policy making in The Netherlands from the past to the present and to draw some conclusions. But before reviewing the past, we will explain the position of industrial policy in The Netherlands.

THE POSITION OF INDUSTRIAL POLICY IN THE NETHERLANDS

The concern of government towards industry has of course to do with the important role industry fulfils in the economy. In the first place the importance of industry within the economy is expressed by the contribution it makes to national income and employment. To both the contribution is about 20 per cent. In the second place the importance of industry is reflected in its contribution to exports. Two-thirds of total exports are industrial. In the third place industry generates knowledge which is often also of use in other business sectors. In the fourth place industry is an important main contractor. The interdependence between industry and the service sector is becoming stronger; indeed, to an increasing extent industry outsources certain activities to the service sector.

Government policy, which has the aim of safeguarding industrial competitiveness, takes the form of a two-edged razor. In the first place it concerns policies which generally favour conditions for industrial development, that is to say the security of a sound infrastructure, low tax burdens and high-quality education. In the second place, it concerns policies which deliberately favour industrial interests, that is facilitating the adjustment of industry to changing conditions at the micro, meso and macro levels of the economy.

In The Netherlands the following arguments are maintained to justify designated industrial policy:

. infant industry argument, which means that government is allowed to support large-scale projects which would otherwise never have been implemented. This is either because such projects need mammoth investment or because firms cannot carry the risks involved;
. matching, which occurs when government pursues a policy of financial support because foreign governments do the same;
. positive external effects, which point to the fact that the production of knowledge by means of R&D can have certain spillover effects to other firms instead of being only of benefit to the originating firm;
. insufficient information. Although a well-known feature of the neoclassical model of the economy is the supposed availability of all necessary information, in real life insufficient information is a fact.

Small and medium sized enterprises in particular have to cope with this feature;
. imperfections in complementary markets, which can be illustrated by the case of the capital market. If there is a lack of sufficient access to high-risk venture capital, government intervention can be directed at offering credits for technological development or giving a guarantee on high-risk venture capital offered by financial institutions;
. the existence of learning curves, which means that the uncertainties involved in early R&D activities may hinder firms from undertaking them.

HISTORICAL REVIEW OF THE DUTCH ECONOMIC SITUATION

In order to determine the role of industrial policy in The Netherlands in relation to the industrial transformation process, we will make a brief historical excursion starting at the end of World War II and ending at the beginning of the nineties.

1945-1963: Post-War Reconstruction and Expansion

The post-war industrial policy is mainly characterised by industrial reconstruction. The government votes eight 'industrialisation bills', of which the last one, in 1963, contains targets which are only indicative in character. In the immediate post-war years an important role is ascribed to government, as far as industrial reconstruction is concerned. The establishment of the Central Planning Bureau is a result of this line of thought. Later cabinets turn away from this 'plan-rational' orientation. Government's role is limited to creating conditions which foster economic development. Industry itself is considered responsible for deciding upon investments and production.

The Sixties: Turbulent Growth

Economic development within the sixties can be regarded as extremely favourable. As wealth and wages increase, there is some erosion of the political and social consensus which had underlain the early stages of post-war reconstruction and expansion. Disagreement relates to such issues as wages and working conditions, income distribution and social insurance coverage. Up to the first oil shock there is also a debate on environmental affairs.

In line with this discussion a governmental paper is published in 1966 which embodies a renewed emphasis on government intervention. According to this paper the expansion of high-tech, non-polluting industries is to be encouraged. However, as a consequence of the fall of the cabinet in 1966, the influence of this paper is not large.

It can be held that in the post-war period, until the end of the sixties, industrial policy as such did not have an important role to play. General economic policy was able to create the conditions necessary for sound economic development. A more 'plan-rational government orientation' was sometimes discussed, but never really established. In the seventies, however, we do see a shift towards a bigger role for a designated industrial policy.

The Seventies: Recession

During the seventies government realises that a large number of firms have neglected the necessity for structural adjustment. Within the context of sector restructuring plans, the NEHEM (Dutch Society for Reconstruction) is established to coordinate these processes. To overcome the steep rise in unemployment, government starts off with employment programmes. As the situation worsens after 1973, support for individual firms becomes predominant. This kind of support is justified on the ground that the difficulties of many enterprises are related to the depth of the recession and that those enterprises are viable in the long term. Between 1975 and 1980 three billion guilders is spent on support for individual firms.

The Eighties: Recovery

From the early 1980s resources are shifted away from defensive support towards a more forward-looking stance. Measures to encourage 'selective growth' are largely abandoned, the number of programmes and their level of support reduced, and procedures for obtaining government aid and approval for investment simplified. Industrial policy is focused on technological innovation. Support is given to R&D carried out by firms, mainly individual firms.

From the mid-eighties industrial policy assumes a more dynamic stance. It not only recognises the importance of technological innovation as such, but also the potential chain effects created *inter alia* by scientific and entrepreneurial activities. This leads to the establishment of four national technology programmes. Support is given to R&D activities at different stages in technology trajectories of highly pervasive technologies. Also, more attention is paid to the dissemination of knowledge already generated. The establishment of a network of innovation centres is one of the outcomes of this policy line. The recognition of the importance of value chains of production within industrial sectors is translated into a programme which stimulates subcontracting.

The Nineties: Industrial Transformation and Industrial Policy

As we are now in a period of industrial transformation, designated industrial policy attracts a lot of attention. This attention has been triggered by the fact that the control over two important Dutch enterprises has recently passed into foreign hands. The fear is that the future of these industrial centres of excellence will be at stake if they are left to the fate of foreign control. The debate focuses on the requirements that industrial policy should meet in order to keep high tech, upgraded industrial activities in our country. Policy lines (which can be classified as policy which fits into the industrial dynamics tradition) receive a great deal of attention and acclaim.

The internationalisation of the world economy is increasing. The unification of the European market and the resulting increased competition which became apparent in the mid eighties imply the growth of international trade and direct foreign investment. Rapid technological developments imply the shortening of product life cycles. As a consequence R&D costs expand enormously. Networks and cooperation between firms are induced by the high costs and risks involved.

The trend towards rapid internationalisation and expanding R&D costs compel firms to pursue scale enlargement not only by means of investment, but also by buy-outs. Business activities are becoming footloose. The current trend among major players in strategically sensitive sectors is to strengthen their competitive position, share the burden of R&D costs and gain a foothold in foreign markets via a web of joint ventures, cooperative agreements and the like. Economic activities on the one hand and corporate control on the other are diverging.

Apart from the fact that the emergence of transnational corporations has shown to impair the effectiveness of sector- or technology- specific national support policies, the simple fact that company networks no longer stop at the frontiers of a country reduces this cause for concern. To an increasing extent, however, it is considered important that in terms of the industrial transformation process, Dutch companies have an equal starting point in comparison with foreign companies. With regard to this need for equality we do have some worries. First of all, we have a rather small home market in comparison with other European countries. This implies that the scale of our medium-sized companies is often smaller than that of their European competitors. In the second place, bigger European countries have enhanced financial possibilities to bring their companies into a better competitive position. Financial support for Dutch industry in terms of a percentage of GNP is much smaller than elsewhere within the EC. In the third place, the governments of several other European countries are taking an active role in looking after the interests of their industry. In some cases they protect it from take-overs by acting as a majority shareholder in national companies. Also cross shareholding by banks and other companies is being stimulated.

In addition to government policies which generally favour conditions which are conducive to entrepreneurship, the present situation reveals that some designated industrial policy activities are necessary. Clusters of subcontractors, research institutes and customers have become concentrated around different core industries. Cooperation between the different parties within these clusters is necessary to meet the high costs and risks involved in R&D. Solid cooperation will safeguard such high tech industrial activities. The government therefore wants to strengthen this cooperation.

The programme 'Subcontracting and Outsourcing', which is currently in progress at the Dutch Ministry of Economic Affairs, is a good example of an instrument aimed at stimulating cooperation between companies. Dutch main contractors and subcontractors acknowledge, of course, the strategic importance of networks. Nevertheless, forms of cooperation such as co-makership are not without problems. Particularly difficult are the risks of jointly developing know-how and applying this to new products. The programme therefore promotes cooperation between main contractors and subcontractors in the field of technology and product development. Support is given to projects in eight product market combinations: aerospace, audio-visual productions, automobile industry, telecommunication and office automation, energy and offshore, IC technology, defence industry and machine-engineering. The importance of co-makership within these specific product market combinations has been the major reason to focus the programme on them. The programme aims at facilitating the shift in these sectors from standard deliveries to supply based on the specifications of the client.

Scientific and technological infrastructure can be regarded as the bedrock for a strong competitive industry. Activities of research institutes should therefore be attuned to the requirements of companies. Better cooperation between the two parties will help Dutch industry to solve its R&D problems. A strong market-oriented scientific and technological infrastructure will also attract foreign investment. The government will therefore give support to increased cooperation between research institutes and companies.

The National Technology Programmes, which are in progress at the Ministry of Economic Affairs, give special attention to projects in which companies and research institutes cooperate in R&D. The programmes focus on four fields of technology, namely information technology, material technology, environmental technology and biotechnology. Support for cooperation within these fields is spurred by the fact that chain effects created in technological innovation (*inter alia* by scientific and entrepreneurial activities) also ensure the dissemination of knowledge thus generated.

Another problem which occurs is the more or less insufficient supply of high-risk venture capital. At the same time high tech firms endeavour to keep up in the global technology race. Therefore, the initiative has been taken to create a financial facility in order to enlarge the supply of high-risk venture capital. Discussions with financial institutions have ensured joint responsibility for this instrument from the private sector and government.

CONCLUSION

Looking back on the post-war period, we can recognise growing attention being paid to industrial policy which is in line with the process of industrial transformation. Two important trends which characterise this industrial transformation are the advance of global competition and technological innovation.

In response to the industrial transformation process, the leading philosophy has been that general economic policy has to create the conditions necessary for sound economic development. To safeguard or strengthen high tech industries, attention has been given to the establishment and maintenance of policies and institutions that support and create the conditions which are conducive to entrepreneurship; these include attractive fiscal measures, flexibility in the labour market, high-quality technical education and a solid physical infrastructure.

In addition to this general economic policy stance, some kind of government targeting industrial and technology policy was justified in an economic environment where markets did not function perfectly. Starting with the recession of the seventies and until the mid-eighties, industrial policy has mainly been derived from conceptions which stem from the industrial organisation tradition, that is to say, giving support to individual firms.

The characteristics of the industrial transformation process after the mid-eighties have intensified the necessity for broader framework setting policies. The Dutch government has therefore given increasing attention to industrial interdependence in the sense of network relationships. Vertical integration in industry as a means of internalising externalities and giving the sectors concerned an added competitive edge has become of major importance. Also, the activities of research institutes are regarded as an important input for a strong competitive industry. Policy instruments have therefore been focused on intensifying cooperation between research institutes and companies. These new lines in industrial policy making are closely linked to concept within the industrial dynamics tradition.

REFERENCES

Carlsson, B. (1989), *Industrial Dynamics: Technological, Organizational, and Structural Changes in Industries and Firms*. Dordrecht: Kluwer Academic Publishers.

Dahmen, E. (1984), 'Schumpetrian Dynamics: Some Methodological Notes', *Journal of Economic Behavior and Organization*, 5 (1), 25.

George, K.D. and C. Joll (1981), *Industrial Organisation: Competition, Growth and Structural Change*. London: George Allen & Unwin Ltd.

Johnson, Ch. (1982), *MITI and the Japanese Miracle: The Growth of Industrial Policy, 1925-1975*. Stanford: Stanford University Press.

Soete, L. (1991), 'National Support Policies for Strategic Industries: The International Implications', in *Strategic Industries in a Global Economy: Policy Issues for the 1990s*. Paris: OECD International Futures Programme.

Index